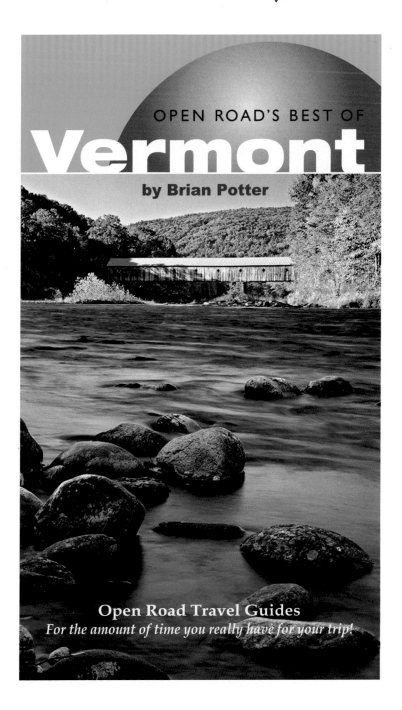

OPEN ROAD'S BEST OF

Vermont

by Brian Potter

Open Road Travel Guides
For the amount of time you really have for your trip!

For more information on Jeff Newcomer's beautiful photos on these first three pages, see page 239.

Open Road Publishing

Open Road's new travel guides cut to the chase. You don't need a huge travel encyclopedia – you need a *selective guide* to steer you right. If you're going on vacation for a few weeks or less, get a guide that brings you the *best* of any destination for the amount of time you *really* have for your trip!

Open Road – the guide you need for the trip you want.

The New Open Road *Best Of* Travel Guides.
Right to the point.
Uncluttered.
Easy.

Open Road Publishing
P.O. Box 284, Cold Spring Harbor, NY 11724
www.openroadguides.com

Text Copyright©2010 by Brian Potter
- All Rights Reserved -
ISBN 13: 978-1-59360-135-5
ISBN 10: 1-59360-135-2
Library of Congress Control No. 2009924895

About the Author
Brian Potter is also the author of *Open Road's Best of New York City*.

Acknowledgments
To the Potter and Schilling families; to Alex, Meg, Rose and Tania; and to my wife, Jamie, with whom Vermont will always have special meaning.

For photo credits turn to page 238.

CONTENTS

1. INTRODUCTION

I've visited **Vermont** countless times over the years, and it gets harder to leave each time. From the mountain vistas along the arterial highways to the textures of the weathered clapboard houses along winding dirt roads, the entire state has a particular beauty – and an ineffable energy – that makes it unlike any place else. If you've never been to Vermont before, suffice to say you're in for a treat.

Vermont's beauty runs deep. Its bright blue lakes reflect many-splendored mountains and forests. Covered bridges span clear-running streams. A lone green-shuttered inn sits at the crest of a hill. These are the images that define a Vermont vacation.

Yet every trip here reveals a new discovery. A back road leads past a farm stand, and all of a sudden your senses are stirred by deep-hued berries, crated apples and fresh-baked scents. Inn-provided snowshoes lead to a novel woodland romp. Raw materials – goldenrod and thistle, maple and cheddar, granite and slate – become stunning in their everyday abundance. Few other destinations offer such richness and variety, and even fewer have such good-hearted people.

Endless beauty, endless variety and ease of life are all Vermont hallmarks. The Green Mountain State has cosmopolitan centers; miles of ski slopes and hiking trails; world-class resorts, cozy lodges and fine dining galore. Whether you're a return visitor or you're brand new to Vermont, this book will show you how to get the most out of your trip. Custom-designed one-day, weekend and weeklong plans have been tailored to suit any time frame. Whether you're here

for culture or the outdoors, romance or a family vacation, this book will help you discover the best that Vermont has to offer.

2. OVERVIEW

Vermont's name comes from the French *verts monts* meaning "green mountains." Once you see its tree-blanketed peaks, rolling hills and verdant valleys, you'll agree that the description fits.

Commanding New England's northwest corner, Vermont is bounded by Canada to the north, New York State to the west, New Hampshire to the east and Massachusetts to the south. All told, Vermont is 9,613 square miles, making it the fifth smallest state.

Unlike the other New England states, Vermont has no Atlantic coastline, but **Lake Champlain** is the largest non-Great Lake in the country and makes up half of the state's western boundary. Another major waterway, the **Connecticut River**, rushes along the state's eastern bor-

der and is the longest river in New England.

In terms of roads, **Interstates 89 and 91** are the major thoroughfares running north to south throughout the state. I-91 runs northward from Brattleboro all the way to the Canadian border while I-89 makes its way from White River Junction northwest to Burlington and beyond.

Routes 2, 4 and 9 run east to west and connect major towns in the southern, central and northern parts of the state, respectively. The following sections break down the major features and attractions of each area so you'll know exactly what to do when you get there.

Southern Vermont

Bookended by **Brattleboro** and **Bennington**, Vermont's lower corners are layered with historic towns, small villages and green hills galore. The **Marlboro Music Festival** and other seasonal highlights take center stage in summer, and resorts such as **Mount Snow** and **Stratton** lure snowbirds in winter. Versatile **Manchester**, the gateway to the Green Mountains, has been popular with travelers for centuries owing to its historic town center, adjoining consumer district and the Equinox Hotel, one of the most fabled resorts in America. Other area attractions include classic villages like **Grafton, Dorset** and **Hildene**, the historic Lincoln family homestead outside Manchester.

Central Vermont

Known for its rugged landscapes and quintessential small towns, central Vermont is a vacation wonderland with something for everyone, whether you're a ski enthusiast, a history buff or just someone in search of a low key, country retreat. **Woodstock** is a refined small-town paradise that's been a tourist destination for centuries, and a number of serious ski resorts – including the biggest of all, **Killington** – offer some of the best outdoor sports anywhere in the northeast. Natural wonders in the region include **Killington Peak, Quechee Gorge** and the **Green Mountain National Forest**.

Northern Vermont

Home to Vermont's tallest mountain, largest lake and biggest city, northern Vermont is an outsized vacation destination that's among the most beautiful (and underrated) in the country. In addition to outdoor icons like **Mount Mansfield** and **Lake Champlain**, the north is home to **Burlington**, Vermont's cosmo-

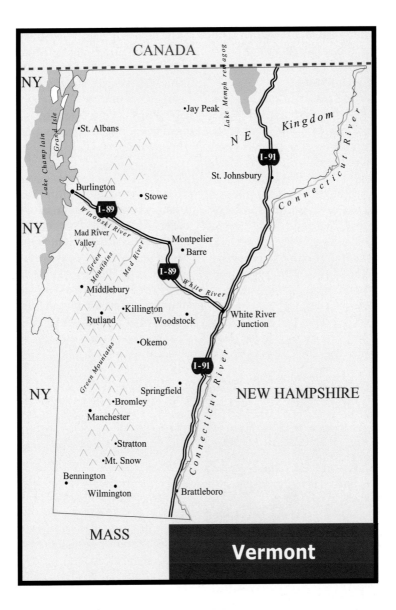

CANADA

NY

Lake Memph re agog

Jay Peak

St. Albans

N E Kingdom

Lake Champlain

Grand Isle

Connecticut River

I-91

St. Johnsbury

Burlington

I-89

Stowe

NY

Winooski River

Mad River Valley

Montpelier

Barre

Green Mountains

Mad River

I-89

White River

Middlebury

Killington

Rutland Woodstock

White River Junction

Okemo

Green Mountains

Connecticut River

I-91

NY

Springfield

NEW HAMPSHIRE

Bromley

Manchester

Stratton

Mt. Snow

Bennington

Connecticut River

Wilmington

Brattleboro

MASS

Vermont

politan center; the storied resorts of **Stowe**; the state capital, **Montpelier**; and the wide open wilderness that is known as the **Northeast Kingdom**.

The Outdoors

Among Vermont's primary allures is its unspoiled, year-round opportunities for connecting with nature. The famous Green Mountains form a spine running nearly the entire length of the state, and there are hundreds of thousands of acres of protected forest and state and national parkland. By itself, the **Green Mountain National Forest** encompasses 850,000 acres and 900 miles of trails.

Classic hiking can be found all along the famous **Long Trail**, which runs 264 miles the length

of the state and includes a segment of the Appalachian Trail. From challenging Mount Mansfield to the leisurely **Stowe Recreation Trail**, hikes of all natures and skill levels can be found up and down Vermont. The Green Mountain Club maintains many of these trails and is a great resource for learning all about them.

Vermont's tallest mountains are **Mount Mansfield, Killington Peak** and **Camel's Hump**, in that order. They and a number of other peaks – from **Mount Snow** in the south to **Jay Peak** in the north – offer the best skiing on the east coast as well as myriad other mountain pursuits, including snowboarding, mountain biking, gondola rides and alpine slides.

Vermont's outdoors are not all remote mountaintops and backwoods trails, however. Lake Champlain, in the state's northwest corner, provides beaches, scuba diving and all manner of water sports, and there are more than **800 lakes and ponds** scattered across the state. Resorts like Killington offer groomed trails, golf courses and other first-class amenities. Many inns and bed and breakfasts offer beautiful grounds that are as ideal for wandering as for admiring from a rocking chair on the porch.

And New Englanders' favorite autumn pursuit – **leaf peeping** – can be done nearly as well from your car as on foot.

Whatever your pleasure, you'll find Vermont's outdoor options are without equal. Each chapter in this book offers the best variety of activities to suit your needs.

Arts & Culture

Burlington is Vermont's largest city and cosmopolitan center, with fine art, theater, a vibrant dining scene and the **University of Vermont** campus contributing to a wide range of cultural possibilities. The **Brattleboro area** is southern Vermont's answer to Burlington, and it also features an array of arts-related activities, from craft markets to galleries to music festivals. Even the smallest towns in Vermont often have a special museum or performing arts venue. Highlights include the **Shelburne Museum** outside Burlington; the **Dorset Playhouse** near Manchester; and **Bread and Puppet Theater** in the Northeast Kingdom.

One of the best things about Vermont, though, is that you don't have to go to a show or to a museum to experience its culture. Quintessential Vermont is completely realizable at the local level, in the people you meet, the foods you eat and the farm-land rolled out before you. For culture in its richest, most basic sense, consume regional delicacies such as maple syrup and cheese; visit general stores, farm stands, bookstores and breweries; and interact with the folks who run them.

You won't find more welcoming people anywhere else in the country. The entire population takes a relaxed sort of pride in their state. While Vermonters are not numerous – only Wyoming and Alaska have smaller populations – they love living here and in many cases wouldn't think of living anywhere else. The whole of Vermont feels like a community, and its open-minded, **live-and-let-live ethos** is enthusiastically followed by liberals and libertarians alike.

Nightlife & Entertainment

While far from a party-first destination, Vermont sure knows how to have fun. Resort regions like **Killington** have robust nightlife scenes, and **Burlington** is a lively college town with more than its share of bars, cafes and music venues. The entire state has been at the vanguard of the country's **craft beer renaissance**, and outstanding breweries and wineries are scattered throughout the state. **Performing arts venues** are also numerous, and you're as likely to find a historic theater or a summer music festival at the end of a country road as you are in the major towns.

Shopping

From boutiques to antiques, Vermont boasts a diverse array of commercial attractions perfect for that special purchase. Known for its outlet shopping, **Manchester** is tops among the state's retail centers while **Burlington** and **Woodstock** offer the best downtown, pedestrian-oriented shopping experiences.

Outside the major tourist centers, nearly every town seems to have a quaint Main Street with shops for browsing. **Antiques** and traditional Vermont **delicacies** are sold everywhere from genteel storefronts to roadside stands, and general stores offer a classic New England take on the convenience store and stock all manner of sundries and souvenirs.

Great Eats & Sleeps

Vermont's **hotels and inns** have so much character that you once you settle in you may never want to leave. Many occupy historic buildings and centuries-old homes surrounded by acres of gardens, trails and forestland. They range from rustic and homey to truly luxurious, and most are run by Vermonters with a genuine love for hospitality.

Resort options are also plentiful and offer access to a wide range of amenities, from skiing and golf to spas and first-class din-

INN TIPS

• **Many inns' rates include breakfast**, and some even include dinner. Keep this in mind when considering the cost of a room.
• To preserve their quiet-getaway status, **some inns don't allow children**. Always confirm a family reservation.
• Many finer inns require **multi-night stays**, especially on weekends and during peak seasons. Single-night bookings can sometimes be made within a few days of your stay.

ing. There are resorst, inns and bed-and-breakfasts here for every budget, and a wide array of cabins and campgrounds for those who wish to get even closer to nature.

Dining in Vermont is as diverse as it is delicious. From resort dining rooms to small-town brewpubs, you can get first-rate fare just about anywhere, and there's a refreshing emphasis on locally produced ingredients that shows in the finished product. Refer to the *Best Sleeps and Eats* section of each destination chapter for my best picks.

3. BRATTLEBORO & SOUTHEASTERN VERMONT

HIGHLIGHTS

▲ Brattleboro

▲ Putney

▲ Grafton

▲ Newfane

▲ Covered Bridges

▲ Route 5 & Route 30 Scenic Drives

INTRO

Vermont's southeast corner has a lot going for it. Its cultural capital, **Brattleboro**, is a laid-back, exceedingly livable town nestled between the Connecticut and West Rivers. Charming villages – **Putney**, **Grafton**, **Newfane** (*see photo on page 18*) – dot the countryside, and everything in between, it seems, is green, from rolling hills to cornfield-studded roads to the ethos of the people.

COORDINATES

Brattleboro sits at the confluence of I-91 and Rt. 5. Take Rt. 30 north to **Newfane** and **Grafton**; take Rt. 5 north to **Putney**; and take Rt. 9 west to **Marlboro**. To get to **Mt. Snow**, take 9 west to 100 north.

Naturally beautiful and pleasingly eccentric, Brattleboro and the Lower Connecticut River Valley offers something for everyone, whether you're an outdoor enthusiast or an art lover.

BRATTLEBORO SIGHTS IN A DAY

Compact, culturally adventurous **Brattleboro** straddles the happy medium between small town and city. You can see most, if not all, of it in one day, but it provides more possibilities than some places twice its size.

Exceedingly walkable, shop-lined **Main Street** is everything that streets of that name used to be. Made for strolling, it has a church at one end, the art deco Latchis Hotel at the other and a run of classic brick storefronts in between. Half a day can be whiled away poking in and out of its independent shops and cafés. Counter and consumer culture happily converge here, with used bookstores, record shops and hemp clothiers comfortably coexisting alongside high-end gift stores and galleries.

Artistically-inclined visitors will love it here. Consistently

SIGHTS

SIGHTS

ranked among the top ten small art towns in America, it's chock full of galleries, artisan shops and local arts and crafts vendors. The wares at **Vermont Artisan Design** are among the best, and you'll want to devote part of your afternoon to the underrated **Brattleboro Museum & Art Center** (BMAC). Housed in a nearly century-old rail station (*photo below*), it spotlights local and international artists with an emphasis on the contemporary.

Info: *Vermont Artisan Design*
106 Main St.
Tel. 802-257-7044
www.vtartisans.com
BMAC
10 Vernon St
Open Wed.-Mon. 11 am-5 pm

Admission $4
Tel. 802-257-0124
www.brattleboromuseum.org

Brattleboro's evening options are similarly eclectic. The town's most reliable source of evening entertainment is the **Latchis Theater**. The classic art deco facility hosts New England Youth Theater Company productions as well as a steady stream of popular and art-house films on a trio of screens. Concerts, art exhibitions and the like are also frequently scheduled. And no visit to Brattleboro, however short, is complete without a visit to **McNeill's Brewery**, a rustic local favorite that's been at the vanguard of Vermont's microbrew revolution.

Info: *Latchis Theater*
50 Main St.
Tel. 802-246-1500.
www.latchis.com
McNeill's Brewery
90 Elliot St.
Tel. 802-257-9102

A WEEKEND IN BRATTLEBORO

Some of the area's premier events happen Friday through

Sunday, so a weekend visit expands your options expo-

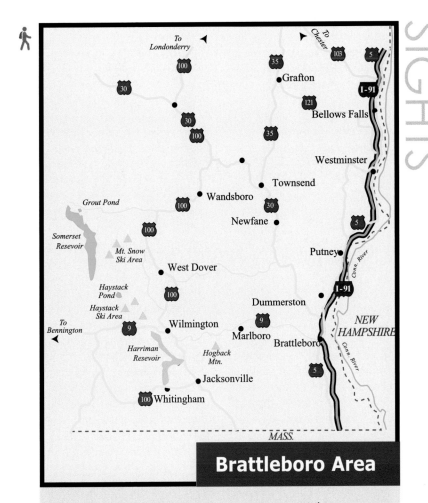

Brattleboro Area

nentially. Explore the **surrounding countryside** a little too. As in any "big city" in Vermont, being downtown means you're just a stone's throw from the great outdoors.

Brattleboro's foremost weekend attraction is the **Brattleboro Farmers' Market**,

a quintessential Vermont experience – exceedingly friendly, colorful and overflowing with fresh food and community spirit. Local vendors offer an array of produce, meats, cheeses and crafts (pottery, knitwear, etc.) as well as prepared meals and treats. Whether you're crav-

SIGHTS

ing pad Thai or chai, picnic supplies or a souvenir stop, a visit to this open-air market is a must.

Info: just off Route 9 past the Creamery Covered Bridge (the only surviving wooden covered bridge in Brattleboro). Open Saturdays, 9am to 2pm, from May to November.

The Brattleboro arts scene is also at its liveliest the first Friday of each month for **Gallery Walk**, the town's premier visual arts event. Tours of over fifty galleries are self-guided (pick up a free booklet with map at participating galleries or simply follow the colored numbers in gallery windows) and feature artist talks and a friendly, festive vibe. Book a restaurant reservation after and make a night of it.

Info: Open 5:30pm-8:30 pm Tel. 802-257-2616 www.gallerywalk.org

The area's weekend music scene is equally vibrant, particularly come summer when the renowned **Marlboro Music Festival** takes center stage. Set on the pastoral Marlboro College campus, just 12 miles west of Brattleboro, the legendary chamber music festival – the premier event of its kind in North America – features a series of hotly-anticipated weekend concerts throughout July and August. Pairing a veritable who's who of the classical world with up-and-coming young musicians, Marlboro is a must for any music lover. As their numbers are many, be sure to book tickets in advance. Jen, the Marlboro box office manager, is a miracle worker, but you

LUNCH AT THE COOP

Across the street from the Brattleboro Museum & Art Center is a local icon: the **Brattleboro Food Cooperative**. Bright, friendly and stocked with all manner of food staples and snacks (and an epic stash of local beer and wine), stop in to pick up a fresh smoothie or a prepared meal from the deli counter – the Co-op's spicy quesadillas (big enough for two) and sides can hang with most restaurants' best. *Info: 2 Main St. Open Mon.-Sat. 8am-9pm, Sun. 9am-9pm.*

don't leave experiences this important to chance.

Info: Off Route 9, Marlboro
Tel. 802-254-2394 (June 20 - Aug. 15) or 215-569-4690
Tickets $5-$35
Programs announced one week in advance
www.marlboromusic.org

A day downtown (as per the Brattleboro one-day plan) plus these special events is nearly a weekend unto itself. Forgoing any of them, however, provides an opportunity to explore the beautiful country on Brattleboro's periphery.

The Connecticut River affords opportunities for **boating, canoeing** and **kayaking**. Rent a vessel from the Vermont Canoe Touring Center, take a narrated river cruise on the "Belle of Brattleboro" tour boat or simply stroll alongside the Connecticut via the walkway running from downtown parallel to Route 119. Leading across two bridges and the river island, the path also offers access to nearby **Mount Wantastiquet**. From the end of the second bridge, turn left on Mountain Rd. and

from the parking area there, you're just a 10-minute walk from the viewing area overlooking the river. If you're feeling ambitious, another 45-minute climb will bring you to the summit.

Info: Vermont Canoe Touring Center
451 Putney Rd.
Tel. 802-257-5008
Belle of Brattleboro departs from Vermont Marina, 28 Springtree Rd.
Tel. 802-254-1263

For further green mountain views, travel the **Molly Stark Trail** west to **Hogback Mountain**. A winding two-lane road cut through verdant hills, this scenic byway (also known as Route 9) offers classic countryside views culminating at **Mt. Olga** and the Hogback Moun-

SIGHTS

tain Visitor Center. About 45 minutes from Brattleboro, the Hogback overlook affords breathtaking wide-horizon views of three states. Also on the premises are a gift shop, information center and the **Southern Vermont Natural History Museum**, which features an extensive collection of local wildlife – some alive, some stuffed.

Info: *Southern Vermont Natural History Museum*
Rte. 9
Open 10am-5pm late May-late Oct; weekends in winter

Admission $5
Tel. 802-464-0048
www.vermontmuseum.org

Real deal animals still roam the pastures of the **Robb Family Farm** five miles from Brattleboro. The pretty, tourable grounds can be traversed by hay ride or sleigh ride and include a country store and a sugarhouse where you can learn about maple production. Popular with families and just a stone's throw from Brattleboro, it's worth a quick jaunt on your way in or out of town.

ALTERNATIVE PLAN

Just 20 miles west of Brattleboro, **Mount Snow** is southern Vermont's most accessible outdoor resort. Running a close second to the Green Mountains in the appropriateness of name category, it's at its best in winter when its nearly 600 skiable acres are blanketed in powder. However, you can have an amazing weekend here without ever strapping on skis. The **Grand Summit Hotel** is a first-

class resort with elegant dining and spa services; hiking and mountain biking are popular pursuits; and whitewashed **Wilmington**, with its flowered window boxes and classic country store, offers quaint lodging options and free bus service to the mountain. *Info*: *Mount Snow Resort, 39 Mt. Snow Rd., W. Dover. Tel. 802-464-3333. www.mountsnow.com.*

Info:
827 Ames Hill Rd.,
West Brattleboro.
Open Mon.-Tues., Thurs.-Sat.

10am-5pm, Sun. 1-5 pm.
Rides $7, $5 for children
Tel. 888-318-9087
www.robbfamilyfarm.com

SIGHTS

A WEEK IN SOUTHEASTERN VERMONT

After a couple of days in and around Brattleboro, it's time to venture further into Vermont. **Small towns of considerable charm** are spread throughout the Lower Connecticut and West River Valleys, and the beauty of the countryside makes driving a delight. Farmstand sightings are frequent, as are opportunities to sample some of the region's best cheese and maple syrup. Classic country stores, antique shops and village greens also dot the landscape. Explore by day and recharge by night, as each town offers inns as steeped in history as hospitality.

Nine miles to the north up Route 5 is **Putney**. A historic village of 19th century buildings and colorful shops, it blends artistic sensibility with a refreshingly rural vibe. Peruse all manner of locally-made arts and crafts, from jewelry to woodwork to quilts, in

With **35 artisan cheese makers** – from Vermont Shepherd in the southeast to Lake's End in the upper northwest – the **Vermont Cheese Trail** runs the length of the state. Download a trail map from the Vermont Cheese Council's web site (*www.vtfarms.org*), then travel along it, sampling some of the 150+ varieties and meeting cows, goats, sheep and even water buffalo along the way.

TRAVEL THE VERMONT CHEESE TRAIL!

SIGHTS

the brook-bisected downtown or pursue an outdoor adventure on the outskirts. Pick berries or press apples into cider at **Green Mountain Orchards** – they've been in the fruit business for over a century – or seek out a sugarhouse such as **Harlow's** for a glimpse into the alchemy that is maple syrup production. Serious foodies will also want to make a detour to the **Vermont Shepherd Cheese Store**. *The New York Times* recently ranked their raw sheep's milk reserve among the nation's best.

Info:
Green Mountain Orchards
130 W. Hill Rd.
Open daily 9:30am-5:30pm
Closed Mon. in winter
Tel. 802-387-5851
www.greenmtorchards.com
Harlow's Sugarhouse
563 Bellows Falls Rd.
Open daily March-Dec.
Tel. 802-387-5852

www.vermontsugar.com
Vermont Shepherd Cheese
281 Patch Farm Rd.
Open daily 9am-5pm
Tel. 802-387-4473
www.vermontshepherd.com

The ride northeast from Putney on **Route 5** becomes increasingly scenic, meandering through farmland and past a number of covered bridges. Pursue the scenery up past Bellows Falls to Chester, then loop back down to **Grafton**, one of the most beautiful, best preserved historic villages in all of Vermont. Authentic from its dignified white church down to its blacksmith shop and welcoming general store, Grafton's also home to a wealth of antique shops, art galleries and classic inns like the elegantly restored **Old Tavern**.

As renowned as it is for colonial atmosphere, however, Grafton may be most famous for its cheese. The **Grafton Village Cheese Company** has been churning out cheddar here since the late 1800s, and you can observe its time-tested cheese crafting process (and sample the results) at the flagship shop just a half-mile from the town center.

Info: 533 Townshend Rd.
Open Mon.-Fri. 9am-5pm, Sat.-
Sun. 10am-5pm
Tel. 800-472-3866
www.graftonvillagecheese.com

Weekend visitors to Grafton can also take advantage of the **Nature Museum's** exhibits, walking trails and wildlife garden while serious outdoor types will want to explore the **Grafton Ponds Outdoor Center's** 50+ miles of trails. Also ripe for exploration are a pair of nearby covered bridges – the Hall Covered Bridge off Rte. 121, just a few miles from Bellows Falls, and the Kidder Hill Covered Bridge at the junction of Routes 35 and 121.

Info: Nature Museum of Grafton
186 Townshend Rd.
Open Sat.-Sun. 10 am-4 pm
Admission $4
Tel. 802-843-2111
www.nature-museum.org
Grafton Ponds Outdoor Center
783 Townshend Rd.
Tel. 802-843-2400
www.graftonponds.com

Halfway between Grafton and Brattleboro are the villages of **Newfane** and **Townshend**. The drive on Route 30 northwest from Brattleboro takes you past

the **West Dummerston Covered Bridge** – at 280 feet the longest covered bridge in Vermont – and, 12 miles on, to Newfane, a quintessentially quaint New England town. The entire village is on the National Register of Historic Places and is full of old houses, churches and age-old character. Outdoor possibilities are plentiful, from the **hiking trails** in Newfane Town Forest to the **swimming holes** along the West and Rock Rivers to the blooming fields of **Olallie Gardens flower farm**. Bargain hunters also won't want to miss the **Newfane Flea Market**, held Sundays along Route 30 a mile north of town. Just be prepared to rise early – shopping starts at 6am sharp.

Info: Olallie Gardens
129 Augur Hole Rd.,
South Newfane
Tel. 802-348-6614

SIGHTS

SIGHTS

Five miles further up Route 30, at its junction with Route 35, Townshend also features plenty of **antiquing** options (more than two dozen stores in all) and **covered bridge** access (the classic, lattice style

STROLLING OF THE HEIFERS

Brattleboro's answer to Pamplona's Running of the Bulls, the **Strolling of the Heifers** is one of Vermont's most unique and eagerly anticipated annual events. Farmers, floats, tractors and over 100 cows and barnyard animals make the stroll down Main Street the first weekend in June in celebration of the state's dairy history.

Festivities continue all weekend long with farm tours, a grilled cheese cook-off and the crowning of the **Miss VermOOnt** prize heifer. **Info**: www.strollingoftheheifers.com.

Scott Covered Bridge on Route 30). The family-owned **Peaked Mountain sheep dairy farm** is another must for cheese hounds, and there's a wealth of outdoor options here too. Townshend Lake offers swimming and – rare for Vermont – a sandy beach while **Townshend State Park** boasts some of the area's best hiking. The trail up Bald Mountain climbs over 1,000 feet past waterfalls to wide-ranging views of Rattlesnake Mountain and the surrounding countryside.

Info: Peaked Mountain Farm 1541 Peaked Mountain Rd. Tel. 802-365-4502 www.peakedmountainfarm.com Townshend State Park 2755 State Forest Rd. Tel. 802-365-7500

BEST SLEEPS & EATS

BRATTLEBORO

Spirit Hill Farm $$$

One of the most romantic lodging spots in southern Vermont, this working llama farm 10 miles west of Brattleboro offers beauty  and privacy in equal measure. The family run property's lone guest quarters are in a rustic timber frame house. The cottage-style suite has its own entrance, fireplace and deck, and while there's no television or internet, who needs them when you have an outdoor hot tub and breakfast delivered right to your door? *Info: www.spirithillfarm.com. Tel. 802-254-6829. 137 Hale Rd. 1 room.*

40 Putney Road Bed & Breakfast $$-$$$

Within walking distance of downtown, this B&B overlooking the West River and the Hogle Wildlife Sanctuary is the most elegantly cozy in the area. Dating to 1929, it features comfortably-appointed rooms and particularly welcoming common areas. Curl up with a book in the tin-ceilinged conservatory or with a pint hearthside at the on-premises pub. The knowledgeable innkeepers serve a full gourmet breakfast including locally roasted Mocha Joe's coffee. *Info: www.fortyputneyroad.com, Tel. 802-254-6268. 40 Putney Rd. 6 rooms.*

Meadowlark Inn $$-$$$

This fully restored, green-shuttered farmhouse dates to the 19th century, although the mountain views and the rocking chairs on the porch feel timeless. The grounds offer room to roam, and the inn's backyard is certified as a wildlife habitat. Guest rooms have a country

LODGING PRICES IN THIS BOOK

$: Less Than $90
$$: $90-180
$$$: More Than $180

SLEEPS & EATS

feel, particularly the secluded, cabin-like Pine Room with woodburning fireplace and French door style windows. The proprietors have culinary degrees and serve a full breakfast featuring their own homegrown organic produce. *Info: www.meadowlarkinnvt.com. Tel. 802-257-4582. 30 Gibson Rd. at Orchard St. 8 rooms.*

Latchis Hotel $$

In the middle of town, this four-story art deco landmark offers location, value and a glimpse into Brattleboro's past and future. On the National Register of Historic Places, it's a bit worn around the edges, but the city has ambitious restoration plans that will eventually transform the property into a multipurpose hotel-arts center anchoring downtown. Until then, guests will continue to appreciate the Latchis's no-frills charm and ample on-site entertainment, from the Flat Street brewpub to the old-fashioned big screen cinema. *Info: www.latchis.com. Tel. 802-254-6300. 50 Main St. 30 rooms.*

Holiday Inn Express $$

The best of the area chains, this clean, convenient Holiday Inn outpost offers a reliable night's sleep a stone's throw from the highway. The fairly new rooms are spacious and fitted with microwaves, flat screen televisions and wireless access. Rates

NAULAKHA
Best known for writing *The Jungle Book*, author **Rudyard Kipling** lived in Vermont from 1892-96. Today his former mansion in Dummerston is a National Historic Landmark that can be rented for stays of three days to three weeks. The four-bedroom house is set on 55 protected acres and includes a museum, study and original Kipling family furnishings. *Info: Tel. 802-254-6868, www.landmarktrustusa.org.*

include a light breakfast. *Info: www.hiexpress.com. Tel. 877-863-4780. 100 Chickering Dr. 86 rooms.*

Whetstone Inn $
Convenient to the Marlboro Music Festival, this family-owned inn offers both charm and affordability. Its comfortably old-fashioned rooms are adorned with books and antiques (but no televisions) and are available with shared or private bath. Breakfast and dinner are both served (at additional cost) in the fireplaced dining room, and a tranquil pond beside the inn highlights the natural beauty of the surroundings. *Info: www.whetstoneinn.com. Tel. 802-254-2500. 550 South Rd., Marlboro. 11 rooms.*

Peter Havens $$$
Personal service, artful surroundings and a menu of traditional favorites characterize Brattleboro's best downtown restaurant. The menu's half dozen entrees focus on seafood and creative meat dishes such as roast duck sauced with sour cherries, currants and port. Decorated with plants and striking artwork, the high-ceilinged dining room has but 10 tables and is managed by the owner, Tom, who often reads the nightly specials. *Info: 32 Elliot St. Tel. 802-257-3333. Dinner Tues.-Sat. Reservations recommended. www.peterhavens.com.*

T.J. Buckley's $$$
Behind T.J. Buckley's vintage diner setting is Vermont's most intimate – and possibly best – gourmet dining experience. The open kitchen serves four subtly perfect entrees each night to just 20 lucky diners at a time and, with but two seatings each night, reservations are a must. Along with the rarified yet humble atmosphere, the uniquely local

RESTAURANT PRICES IN THIS BOOK

$: Less Than $10/diner
$$: $10-20
$$$: More Than $20

flavors on the menu are astounding, and the presentation and attention to detail are second to none. Vegetables are assembled into flowers and hand-carved into other decorative forms. You might expect such artistry to come at a dear price, and indeed it does; be prepared to pay both well and in cash, as the restaurant doesn't accept credit cards. *Info: 132 Eliot St. Tel. 802-257-4922. Dinner Thurs.-Sun. Seatings at 6:30 and 8:30pm. Reservations recommended.*

Fireworks $$

Brattleboro's premier pizzeria doubles as a cozy, wood-fired bistro. Fireworks cranks out classic margherita and more unusual pies such as fig and prosciutto, and sausage, shellfish and Portuguese-style spaghetti star as entrees. The back patio is a great spot in summer, particularly with the house pale ale specially brewed by Otter Creek. *Info: 73 Main St. Tel. 802-254-2073. Dinner daily. www.fireworksrestaurant.net.*

Top of the Hill Grill $-$$

The best BBQ in Brattleboro dishes out pulled pork and ribs, hickory-smoked brisket and all manner of homemade sides as well as house-brewed root beer and vegan wraps. Wood beams and

checkered tablecloths indoors and picnic tables on the outdoor deck make for inviting atmosphere.*Info: 632 Putney Rd. Tel. 802-258-9178. Lunch and dinner daily Apr.-Oct. www.topofthehillgrill.com.*

Brattleboro Food Co-Op $

This 16,000-foot community owned supermarket is filled with fresh produce and an assortment of prepared meals. Quesadillas, sandwiches, salads and sides are great for a picnic or on the go, and there's a small eating area on-premises too. *Info: 2 Main St. Tel. 802-257-0236. Open daily. www.brattleborofoodcoop.com.*

Chelsea Royal Diner $

Known for its platters and blue plate specials, this classic diner serves three superlative "high end home style" meals daily. Homemade ice cream and breakfast all day are served at the Chelsea's quaint, stool-lined counter and cozy wooden booths.

Info: 487 Marlboro Rd. Tel. 802-254-8399. Breakfast, lunch and dinner daily. www.chelsearoyaldiner.com.

PUTNEY

Ranney-Crawford House $$
Built in the Federal style, this lovingly restored red brick house is set amid beautiful gardens and grounds just a few miles outside town. The innkeepers' talents span carpentry, cooking and cycling, so be sure to try out their hand-charted bike routes and hearty three-course breakfasts. *Info: www.ranney-crawford.com. Tel. 802-387-4150. 1097 Westminster West Road. 4 rooms.*

J.D. McCliment's Pub $$
Serving pub fare with a Scottish flair, J.D.'s is a versatile spot with a sunny deck in summer and woodburning stove in winter. Come here for the pizza, the three-course Saturday dinner menu or live music from Irish to bluegrass. *Info: 26 Bellows Falls Rd. Tel. 802-387-4499. Dinner Tues.-Sun. www.jdmcclimentspub.com.*

Curtis' Barbecue $
A true road food classic, Curtis recently celebrated his 40th season serving barbecued chicken and ribs out of a meadow-parked school bus. Rachael Ray endorsed his spicy sauce as #1 in the country, and whether you trust her or the sign proclaiming Curtis's the "ninth wonder of the world," any self-respecting carnivore should try it. Order the distinctively-smoked meats and a homemade birch beer at the bus window, then tear the bones clean at the roadside picnic tables in the yard. Kids also love Curtis's playground and pet pot bellied pig. *Info: I-91, exit 4. Tel. 802-387-5474. Lunch and dinner Tues.-Sun., Apr.-Oct., 10 am-dark. www.curtisbbqvt.com.*

GRAFTON

Old Tavern at Grafton $$$
Among the oldest operating inns in America, the Old Tavern has been refurbished in classic country style by the conservation-oriented Windham Foundation. The three-story columned house – all rustic beams and antiques – features an award-winning

SLEEPS & EATS

dining room (full breakfast included) and 11 guest rooms, with the rest in cottages throughout the property. Guests have free access to the Grafton Ponds Recreation Center along with tennis, trails and – perhaps most alluring of all – the antique rocking chairs on the Tavern's front porch. *Info: www.oldtavern.com. Tel. 802-843-2231. 92 Main St. 46 rooms.*

Inn at Woodchuck Hill Farm $$

Less than 2 miles from the village and slightly off the beaten track, this farmhouse inn can be tricky to find but is well worth the trouble thanks to the hospitality of the innkeepers and the low-key luxury of its barn suites. Wood-paneled, rustic and decorated with antiques, the suites are pricier than regular rooms but worth the splurge. Standard rooms with shared bath deliver good value, and all allow you to enjoy the farm's 200 acres with pond, gazebo and steam room. *Info: www.woodchuckhill.com. Tel. 802-843-2398. Middletown Rd. 7 rooms.*

Old Tavern $$$

As befitting its status as one of the oldest inns in America, the Old Tavern does food the traditional way. Its kitchen garden supplies the produce behind an elegant, locally inspired menu that is always served by candlelight. The main dining room is classy and traditional, and the property offers less formal options as well, including the neighboring Daniels House for light lunchtime fare and the super homey Phelps Barn bar, which serves a light tapas menu and McNeill's beer on weekends. *Info: 92 Main St. Tel. 802-843-2231. Dinner daily, lunch weekends. www.oldtavern.com.*

Moon Dog Café $

Seven miles north of Grafton via Route 35, this colorful coffee shop in an old house on the Chester village green doubles as a market and organic café. Sandwiches, salads and baked goods complement the house-made smoothies, and natural food items and gifts such as soap and jewelry are available to take home. *Info: 287 S. Main St., Chester. Tel. 802-875-4966. Open daily.*

NEWFANE

Four Columns Inn $$$

A columned Greek Revival farmhouse and elegantly restored barn anchor this 150-acre prize property 11 miles north of Brattleboro. Stan-

dard inn rooms are exceedingly cozy with antique furnishings, hardwood floors and fine brass and four poster beds while fireplace suites up the ante with hearthside warmth, extra luxurious baths and French doors that open to mountain views. The colonial décor and rural atmosphere (gardens, brook, pond) may be surpassed only by the breakfast buffet served daily in their James Beard Award-winning restaurant. *Info: www.fourcolumnsinn.com. Tel. 800-787-6633. 21 West St. 15 rooms.*

West River Lodge $-$$

Popular with equestrians – there's also a stable here – this classic farmhouse-style lodge dates to 1820 and features basic accommodations and a comfortable fireplaced living room. Guest rooms with shared bath are a particularly good value, and a country breakfast is included. *Info: www.westriverlodge.com. Tel. 802-365-7745. 117 Hill Rd. 8 rooms.*

Four Columns Inn $$$

This AAA Four Diamond dining room revolves around its central hearth and a classic New England menu accented with Asian and French flourishes. Winner of both James Beard and *Wine Spectator* Awards, it's known for its tender meats, sizable portions and

SLEEPS & EATS

the hospitality you'd expect from one of the very best inns in the region. *Info:21 West St. Tel. 800-787-6633. Dinner daily. www.fourcolumnsinn.com.*

Newfane Market $

The best deli in southern Vermont's been in business since 1825, so its cider donuts, soups and made to order sandwiches come with the weight of tradition behind them. Warm up beside the market's pot bellied stove or with the extensive selection of beer and wine to go. *Info: 596 Vt. Rte. 30. Tel. 802-365-7775. Open daily 7 am-7pm.*

WEST TOWNSHEND
Windham Hill Inn $$$

Setting a new standard for country chic, this top of the line inn is among the most luxurious in Vermont. The expansive grounds include a frog pond, hundreds of acres of forest, meadow and trails and a litany of country club-style recreation options such as clay tennis courts and a brick-terraced swimming pool. The main house's parlors are filled with books, antiques, Oriental carpets and woodburning fireplaces, and the equally luxurious guest rooms include fine furniture, private porches and Jacuzzis. Choose from among classic, loft and fireplace rooms in the main inn or separate but equally comfortable White Barn. *Info: www.windhamhill.com. Tel. 802-874-4080. 311 Lawrence Dr. 21 rooms.*

Windham Hill Inn $$$

The Windham Hill Inn's candlelit dining room is as lavish as its famously luxurious guest rooms. Served in one seating from 6 to 8:30 pm, dinner features a four-course *prix fixe* menu, an even more extensive tasting menu and à la carte options. The *prix fixe* will set you back $60, but with calling card dishes such as tofu Wellington, venison with juniper berries and an amazing Godiva chocolate soufflé, you just might find it worth it. *Info: 311 Lawrence Dr. Tel. 800-944-4080. Dinner daily. www.windhamhill.com.*

MT. SNOW/DEERFIELD VALLEY

Mount Snow Resort $-$$$

Mount Snow's lodging accommodates a variety of budgets and runs the gamut from the deluxe **Grand Summit Resort Hotel** to the relatively spartan **Snow Lake Lodge**. The vast Grand Summit is at the base of the mountain and has everything from studios to multi room suites; all feature comfortable, modern furnishings, and some have full kitchens. The complex includes a sauna, gym, hot tubs and a large outdoor pool that's heated all year round. It's all-encompassing yet can also feel empty off season.

Once the mountain's main lodge, the Snow Lake is also extremely convenient to the slopes, but the similarities end there. Guest rooms are rather dated, and noise can be a concern, but if you're just looking for a place to crash after a long day outdoors, it's a reasonable choice based on price and location. Condo rentals, both on site and off, are another popular option. Snow Resorts is the area's largest rental company, and you can peruse their listings through the resort's web site or by calling 800-245-7669 for comprehensive information. Wherever you stay, be sure to explore the resort's array of ski and stay packages. *Info: www.mountsnow.com. Tel. 800-498-0479. Grand Summit Resort Hotel, 89 Grand Summit Way. 196 rooms. Snow Lake Lodge, 89 Mountain Rd. 92 rooms. Snow Resorts, Tel. 800-245-7669.*

Hermitage Inn $$$

The best of tradition and modern luxury meet at West Dover's Hermitage. The classic 1842 inn underwent a major renovation in 2008. Its 25-acre estate features a trout pond and trails as well as tennis courts and a luxurious outdoor pool. Guest rooms have fireplaces, antiques – and flat screen televisions. Its art collection spans decoys to Delacroix lithographs, and its award-winning restaurant is feted as much for its home-raised game birds as its 2,000 label wine list. *Info: www.hermitageinn.com. Tel. 802-464-3511. 25 Handle Rd., West Dover. 11 rooms.*

SLEEPS & EATS

Inn at Sawmill Farm $$$

Spread across four buildings and 20 acres, the Inn at Saw Mill offers luxurious, estate-style lodging in a classic Vermont farm setting. The 18th century farmhouse still features original beams,

hand-hewn posts and decorative materials such as copper and slate. For even more romance, book a private cottage such as the cozy Wood Shed with fireplace and floor-to-ceiling windows that look out on to the pond. Rates are dear but are inclusive of a full breakfast and five-course dinner in the inn's restaurant, which is among the finest in the state. *Info: www.theinnatsawmillfarm.com. Tel. 802-464-8131. 7 Crosstown Rd., West Dover. 20 rooms.*

Deerhill Inn $$-$$$

Five minutes from Mt. Snow, the Deerhill Inn is the perfect compromise between high-end luxury and a homey B&B. Rates are a little lower than at the estate inns above, but the Deerhill nevertheless offers superlative dining and fine country features. Well-appointed rooms have modern conveniences as well as character, particularly the Lilac Room with periwinkle garden theme and French doors that lead to a balcony. Relaxation opportunities abound throughout the property, whether looking out on to the mountains from the porch, rocking in a chair by the stone fireplace or dining by candlelight. The full breakfast includes the inn's standout home-baked muffins. *Info: www.deerhillinn.com. Tel. 802-464-3100. 14 Valley View Rd., West Dover. 14 rooms.*

Snow Goose Inn at Mount Snow $$-$$$

An area favorite for its understated décor and location just a mile from Mt. Snow, this sprawling white house on three woodland acres splits the difference between country inn and hotel. It's bigger than most of the former but still offers lovely grounds and a robust homemade breakfast featuring house-seasoned bacon. Guest rooms are relatively basic but offer perks such as balconies, woodburning fireplaces and spacious spa tubs. *Info: www.snowgooseinn.com. Tel. 888-604-7964. 259 Rte. 100, West Dover. 32 rooms.*

Deerfield Valley Inn $$
This 1885 country house was the first inn in the Deerfield Valley. On the National Register of Historic Places, it upholds tradition today with reasonable rates, well-appointed rooms (some of which have fireplaces and sitting areas), a full breakfast and afternoon tea. *Info: www.deerfieldvalleyinn.com. Tel. 800-639-3588. 120 Rte. 100, West Dover. 9 rooms.*

Trail's End Inn & Spa $$
This 10-acre property stands out for its peaceful location and on-premises spa and wellness center. Guest rooms range from the merely adequate to deluxe rooms boasting sleigh beds, fireplaces and other luxury amenities. The three-course breakfast starts with house granola, and many packages include dinner. *Info: www.trailsendvt.com. Tel. 802-464-2055. 5 Trails End Ln., Wilmington. 14 rooms.*

Old Red Mill Inn $-$$
The best mix of ambiance and value in the Valley, this inn looks just as the name sounds. The weathered red exterior opens to a rustic parlor and a small restaurant with a lovely porch. Though dated, rooms have charm, and roadside and riverside rates let you choose between ultimate value and peace and quiet. *Info: www.oldredmill.com. Tel. 802-464-3700. 18 N. Main St., Wilmington. 23 rooms.*

Horizon Inn $
This family-owned budget inn on Route 9 bills itself as an upscale motel, as it offers an indoor heated pool and friendly service in addition to clean and comfortable basic rooms. The price is right, as is the location just five minutes from town and 15 minutes from the slopes. *Info: www.horizoninn.com. Tel. 802-464-2131. 861 Rte. 9 East, Wilmington. 28 rooms.*

Mount Snow Resort $-$$$

From the full-service Timber House restaurant to a waffle cabin and burrito joint, Mount Snow Resort offers everything from fast food to fine dining. A marketplace café and bar and grill are in the base lodge; cafeterias and bars prevail around the resort; and a trio of dining options – including pizza from the Snow Barn – are available at the Grand Summit Hotel. Accustom yourself to the reality that everything you eat on-resort will cost more than in the real world. *Info: www.mountsnow.com. Tel. 800-498-0479.*

Inn at Sawmill Farm $$$

From its chandeliers to hand-hewn beams, the Deerfield Valley's most upscale dining room exudes class. Chef Brill Williams's *prix*

fixe dinners include specialties include specialties like Vermont-raised pheasant and a signature dessert of ice cream doused in dark chocolate, butter and nut sauce. The 17,000-bottle wine cellar is an oenophile's dream with a *Wine Spectator* Grand Award winning list of rare vintages going back more than 50 years. *Info: 7 Crosstown Rd., West Dover. Tel. 802-464-8131. Dinner daily. www.innatsawmillfarm.com.*

Two Tannery Road $$$

Once frequented by Teddy Roosevelt, this 17th century home turned high-end dining room boasts a traditional menu and an antique bar from the original Waldorf-Astoria. A Mount Snow institution, they have built their repertoire largely around steaks, seafood and their signature roast Long Island duckling. *Info: 2 Tannery Rd., West Dover. Tel. 802-464-2707. Dinner Tues.-Sun. www.twotannery.com.*

Poncho's Wreck $-$$

A taste of Mexico decidedly north of the border, Poncho's serves everything from fajitas to seafood in its nautically-decorated restaurant and bar. Live entertainment and house margaritas bring the latter alive later in the evening. *Info: 10 S. Main St., Wilmington. Tel. 802-464-9320. Dinner daily, lunch weekends.*

Maple Leaf Malt & Brewing Company $-$$

The Maple Leaf has stopped brewing its own beer, but it still offers a dozen microbrews alongside solid pub fare that includes burgers and sizable portions of ribs. The three-story house on Main Street fills with the après-ski crowd in high season. *Info: 3 N. Main St., Wilmington. Tel. 802-464-9900. Open daily.*

Dot's Diner $

A local treasure for its full-fledged diner counter and friendly, nostalgia-driven atmosphere, Dot's starts serving breakfast at

5:30 am and cranks out first-class comfort food straight through to dinner. The double berry pancakes are morning favorites while the dinner platters and award-winning Jailhouse Chili stand out later in the day. Call ahead when dining at peak times. *Info: 3 W. Main St., Wilmington. Tel. 802-464-7284. Breakfast, lunch and dinner daily.*

SLEEPS & EATS

BEST SHOPPING

Brattleboro

Independent shops and boutiques line **Main Street**, Brattleboro's main drag, and its side streets. Fabulous bookstores, record stores and alternative clothiers comfortably co-exist alongside high-end galleries and gift shops. Shop **Altiplano** (*42 Elliot St.*) and **Vermont Artisan Design** (*106 Main St.*) for arts and crafts; **Twice Upon a Time** (*63 Main St.*) for antiques and vintage clothing; **Tom & Sally's** (*485 West River Rd.*) for handmade chocolate; and **Brattleboro Books** (*34 Elliot St.*) for its 75,000 + books.

Sam's Outdoor Supply (*Flat Street*) is the primary outdoor outfitter, and the **Brattleboro Food Cooperative** (*2 Main St.*) is your best bet for groceries and sundries. The **Brattleboro Farmers' Market** (*off Route 9 near the Creamery Covered Bridge*) also operates on Saturdays 9am-2pm, May-Nov., and is a colorful place to pick up crafts and souvenirs. On Route 9 the **Vermont Country Deli** stocks Vermont specialty foods and gourmet gift baskets.

Putney/Grafton/Newfane

Putney has a lively shopping scene, with a number of artisan shops offering jewelry, woodwork, knit items and other arts and crafts. Townshend and Grafton are both popular for antiquing; try **Riverdale Antiques** (*on Route 30*) or Sylvan Hill Antiques (*35 Eastman Rd. off Route 35 between Grafton and Chester*).

Cheese lovers flock to the **Grafton Village Cheese Company's** flagship shop (*533 Townshend Rd.*) just a half-mile outside town, and you never know what you'll find at the **Newfane Flea Market** (*in a large field just north of Newfane along Route 30*), a seasonal (May-Oct.) shopping adventure every Sunday . It gets started around 6am and runs until 2pm.

Mt. Snow/Deerfield Valley

With locations in the main base lodge and the Grand Summit Hotel, **Mount Snow Sports** is the mountain's prime outdoor outfitter. The villages of the Deerfield Valley (**Wilmington, West Dover**) are home to a variety of historic shops, craft galleries and antique dealers, and maple products can often be found at roadside stands.

BEST NIGHTLIFE & ENTERTAINMENT

Brattleboro

From brewpubs to wine bars to cafes, **Brattleboro** offers a lively yet laid-back nightlife scene. **McNeill's** (*90 Elliot St., Tel. 802-254-2553*) is the first

name in beer, with six house-made drafts (try the Slopbucket brown ale or the Deadhorse IPA) and long wooden tables that encourage community.

Next to the Latchis Hotel, the **Flat Street Brewpub** (*6 Flat St., Tel. 802-257-1911*) also has its share of microbrews (many from the nearby Berkshire Brewing company) as well as a solid list of cocktails and bar fare.

A stop here dovetails well with a movie at the grand old **Latchis movie house** (*50 Main St., Tel. 802-254-6300*). It screens art and commercial

films year round; for a vintage feel, watch from the balcony.

For a different sort of vintage, **Metropolis wine bar** (*55 Elliot St./ 802-254-1221*) and the **Wine Gallery** (*30 Main St., Tel. 802-246-0877*) offer a refined night out with wines by the glass. The latter's casually elegant space along the Whetstone Brook makes it one of Brattleboro's most romantic night spots.

Other popular in-town hangouts include **Mocha Joe's** coffee shop (*82 Main St.*) open till 10 pm on weekends, and the **Mole's Eye** (*4 High St., Tel. 802-257-0771*), a south-of-the-border style pub and concert venue. An eclectic music scene prevails all around town, from the **Weathervane Music Hall** (*19 Elliot St., Tel. 802-258-6529*) to the **Vermont Jazz Center**

(*72 Cotton Mill Hill, Tel. 802-254-9088*) to the **Brattleboro Music Center** (*38 Walnut St., Tel. 802-257-4523*).

Other arts-related options include the **First Friday Gallery Walks** from 5:30-8:30pm (*www.gallerywalk.org*) and performances by the **New England Youth Theater** (*Latchis Theater, Tel. 802-246-6398*) and the **New England Center for Circus Arts** (*76 Cotton Mill Hill, Tel. 802-254-9780*). *Info*: *www.brattleborochamber.org*.

Marlboro/Putney
Come summer, the surrounding countryside comes alive with classical music too, from the **Marlboro Music Festival** (*Tel. 802-254-2394*) – the premier event of its kind in the country – to the smaller-scale

Yellow Barn Festival (*Tel. 802-387-4726*) in Putney.

Mt. Snow/Deerfield Valley
The **Snow Barn** (*South Access and Handle Rds., Tel. 802-464-1100*) is Mount Snow's most popular après-ski spot. From up-and-coming young bands to tribute acts, it offers live music on weekends (with a cover charge) along with cheap draft specials and a hot pizza window for refueling. **Cuzzins** (*in the main base lodge*) is another favorite for live music and late night dancing (*see photo below*), while the **Silo's** casual watering hole (*324 Route 100, Tel. 802-464-2553*) is popular with snowboarders. **Harriman's** (*at the Grand Summit Hotel*) host jazz sets on weekends.

BEST SPORTS & RECREATION

Around Brattleboro

The oak glades of **Fort Dummer State Park** are a great choice for birding and wildlife spotting; to get there, follow South Main Street two miles out of town to Old Guilford Road. Swimming holes around Brattleboro are both popular and plentiful. Two of the best are **Timber Creek Dam** (where you can swim above and below the Green River Covered Bridge) and **Harriman Reservoir** (with sandy beaches and a clothing-optional policy). A good way to find a prime swimming spot is to drive along the river until you see a car or two pulled off on the side of the road.

The **Connecticut River** affords opportunities for canoeing and kayaking. Rent a vessel

BIKING TOURS

One of the most refreshing ways to travel Vermont's country roads is by bicycle. Rent one from a local shop or book a tour through **Bike Vermont**. It offers at-your-own-pace rides that cover 25 to 30 miles daily and stop overnight at local inns. *Info*: Tel. 800-257-2226, www.bikevermont.com.

from **Vermont Canoe Touring Center** (*451 Putney Rd., Tel. 802-257-5008*). A walking path also runs along the river parallel to Route 119 and leads across two bridges and the river island to **Mount Wantastiquet**.

Newfane/Grafton

To the north, **Jamaica**

SPORTS & RECREATION

State Park offers hiking, swimming and camping, all within a half-hour's drive of Brattleboro. The hiking trails in **Newfane Town Forest** are top-notch, as are the swimming holes that abound outside Newfane along the West and Rock Rivers. In Grafton, the **Grafton Ponds Outdoor Center** (*783 Townshend Rd., Tel. 802-843-2400*) is the first name in outdoor recreation. It offers equipment rentals and 50+ miles of trails.

Mt. Snow/Deerfield Valley
Mount Snow's state-of-the-art outdoor facilities encompass skiing, hiking, biking, golf and more. Spread over five mountain faces, its **100+ ski trails** are largely in the intermediate category, though there is a good two-mile novice run along the main face and more advanced ones on the north face. Snowboarding facilities, including the 460-foot long superpipe, are both excellent and extensive.

Once the snow melts, Mt. Snow transforms into a **mountain biking mecca** with a skills course and 45 miles of terrain. The majority of trails are beginner-intermediate level, though lift-accessed trails are for advanced riders only. Hiking trails also suit a variety of skill levels. Depending on your fitness, you can trek to the top of 3,600-foot Mount Snow peak; hike the 2.5-mile Ridge Trail linking Snow and Haystack peaks; or follow the relatively leisurely Deerfield Valley Trail. Prior to departure, check in at the **hiking center** at Grand Summit Resort (*Tel. 802-464-4040*).

4. BENNINGTON, MANCHESTER & THE LOWER GREEN MOUNTAINS

HIGHLIGHTS

▲ Bennington

▲ Manchester

▲ Stratton & Bromley year-round sports

▲ Outlet Shopping

▲ Fly Fishing

▲ Green Mountains hiking

INTRO

From mountains to monuments, from canoeing to crafts, southwestern Vermont is rich in natural and cultural attractions. It's defined by a pair of historic towns – **Bennington** and **Manchester** – and the villages and rolling green countryside that lie in between. Whether you've come to ski, shop or soak up some colonial history, you'll find this to be one of the most beautiful and versatile corners of Vermont.

COORDINATES

Bennington lies at the junction of Routes 7 and 9. **Manchester** is about 25 miles north on Rt. 7A; both **Bromley** (Rt. 11) and **Stratton** (Rt. 30) are very close to Manchester via Rt. 100. **Dorset** is on Rt. 30 and **Arlington** is north of Manchester along Rt. 7A.

SIGHTS

BENNINGTON SIGHTS IN A DAY

Bennington is Vermont's third largest city, but its vibe is more **small town colonial**. A splendid blend of natural beauty and Revolutionary War-era history, its attractions include historic monuments, covered bridges and a quaint, streetlamp-lined shopping district.

Nineteenth century brick buildings frame **Main Street**, and the ghosts of American legends, from Ethan Allen to Robert Frost, haunt its watering holes and cemeteries. This heritage, however, is leavened with a dash of 21st century artistic sensibility. The influence of a number of eclectic galleries, public art projects and the **Bennington College** campus have instilled a refreshing, forward-looking appeal to a town otherwise grounded in the past.

The most pointed proof of Bennington's history is its signature landmark, the **Bennington Monument**. Rising from the town's green-edged fringe, this 306-foot stone obelisk was built to commemorate the 1777 Battle of Bennington (which, minor detail, actually took place six miles to the northwest in New York). Learn about Revolutionary War era exploits at the monument's base, then

SIGHTS

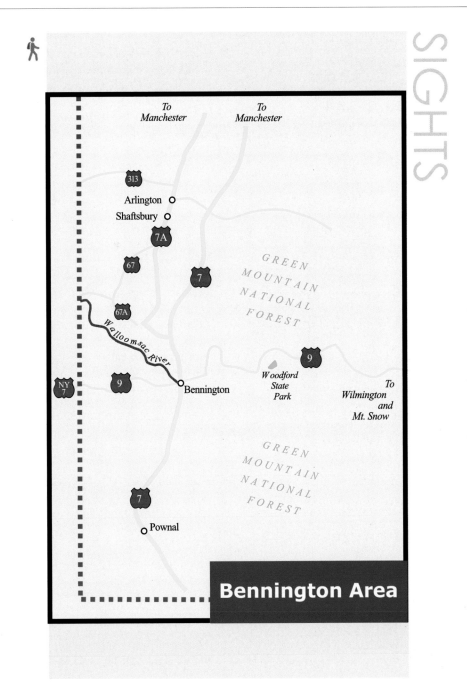

Bennington Area

SIGHTS

with its picket fences and classic Federal style homes. Bell-towered **Old First Church** – the oldest church in Vermont – sits at the crest of the hill and is open to visitors May through October. As the final resting place of the poet **Robert Frost** and a number of Revolutionary War leaders, its adjacent Old Burial Ground also merits some grave consideration.

Just a short walk from the church is the town's premier arts attraction: the **Bennington Museum**. Stocked with all manner of Americana, from fine furniture to glassware, it's best known for holding the largest public collection of Grandma Moses paintings anywhere in the country. Perhaps America's most beloved folk artist, Moses taught herself to paint in her seventies, and her scenes of rural life burst with the simple earnestness of days gone by.

take the elevator up to the **observation platform** for breathtaking views of the town, the Taconic and Green Mountain Ranges and the surrounding states. There's no better way to start your day.

Info: *15 Monument Circle*
Open daily 9am-5pm, mid-April-Oct
Tel. 802-447-0550.
Admission $2

Following this monumental glimpse, head into town to see **Old Bennington** up close. Set on a hilltop, this historic village one mile west of downtown is like a trip back in time

Info: *75 Main St*
Open Thurs.-Tues. 10am-5pm
Tel. 802-447-1571
www.benningtonmuseum.org
Admission $9

Another of the museum's hallmarks is its collection of lo-

SIGHTS

cally produced pottery. If you appreciate the textures and craft in the historic vessels on display, you'll want to head over afterwards to **Bennington Potters**, where the town's flagship artisans still churn out distinctive handmade stoneware as they have for over fifty years. The factory and outlet store are housed in a restored grist mill and schoolhouse building located just off North Street three blocks north of Main.

From the **Potters Yard** you can take an hour-long, self-guided walking tour of the area or simply browse all manner of plates, mugs and bowls, many of which come in distinctive, densely dappled patterns – part Rorschach, part Holstein – that impart a snowflake-like individuality to each piece.

Info: *324 County St*
Open daily
Tel. 800-205-8033
www.benningtonpotters.com
Admission free

Before or after your visit, slake your hunger at the **Blue Benn Diner**. Housed in a vintage 1945 dining car a mere two blocks from the Pottery Yard,

the Blue Benn is a Bennington original known for its old-school ambiance and hearty, affordable comfort food.

Info: *314 North St*
Tel. 802-442-5140

Cap your afternoon with a stroll through Bennington's exceedingly walkable downtown. Peek in some galleries, and stop to admire **historic buildings** such as the Hotel Putnam – it dates to 1873 – the stately marble post office and the Old Stone Mill. Independent bookstores and boutique clothing shops are clustered along Main and North Streets. The sweetest spot on the former is clearly the **Village Chocolate Shop**, which is worth a visit as much for its 82-pound chocolate moose, Benny, as for its treats.

For evening time entertainment, check the schedule at the **Bennington Center for the Arts** – home of the Oldcastle Theatre – or grab a pint at the

Madison Brewing Company
on Main Street.

Info: BCA
44 Gypsy Ln. at Route 9

Tel. 802-447-0564
www.benningtoncenterforthearts.org
Madison Brewing Company
428 Main St
Tel. 802-442-7397

A WEEKEND IN THE MANCHESTER AREA

For an ideal town-centered weekend in southwestern Vermont, split your time more or less equally between Bennington and Manchester. Spend your opening hours in historic **Manchester Village**, in the shadow of **Mt. Equinox**, then head south to **Hildene** – the palatial Lincoln homestead – and on to **Bennington**. The twenty-five miles between Manchester and Bennington are best covered via **scenic Route 7A**, which leads past Hildene and through the villages of Arlington and Shaftsbury.

Manchester has long been a tourist destination as a resort town and gateway to the Green Mountains. Today it has a split personality – part historic village, part shopping capital, part outdoor center – that's key to its appeal.

Situated on the south side of town, **Manchester Village** is the town's most charming spot, a collection of beautifully preserved colonial era buildings centered on the golden-domed Bennington Courthouse, the white-steepled Congressional Church and the historic Equinox Hotel. Stroll the Village's shop-lined streets or opt for the aerial view from the top of Mount Equinox. A five-mile ride from town to summit, panoramic **Skyline Drive** winds its way 3,816 feet to the mountain's summit and affords awe-inspiring views of the surrounding ranges.

Info: Skyline Drive
Open 9 am-dusk
Tel. 802-362-1114

SIGHTS

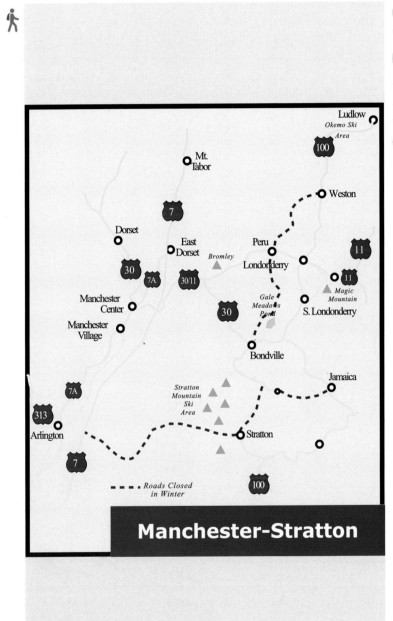

Manchester-Stratton

SIGHTS

Admission $12 per car, $2 per passenger (children under 12 free)

Home to a number of high quality, high-end restaurants and inns, Manchester Village is a worthy place to splurge on a special meal or overnight stay. The classic choice is the storied **Equinox Hotel**.

Built at the base of its namesake mountain, this 183-room inn has hosted numerous dignitaries over the years and, more than a century and a half since its opening, remains the area standard in luxury hospitality. In addition to its opulent guest rooms, the Equinox offers award-winning restaurants and enough outdoor adventures, from archery to falconry, to keep you busy many weekends over.

Info: 3567 Main St
Tel. 800-362-4747
www.equinoxresort.com

Once you've fully explored Manchester Village, head for the hills, where the area's premier historic attraction, **Hildene** (*photo below*) is situated just a couple of miles to the south off Route 7A. Despite its proximity to town, Hildene has the feel of a country estate – which is exactly what Abraham Lincoln's son **Robert Todd Lincoln** built it as around the turn of the century.

The family's summer homestead is a marvel inside and out. Its museum contains an impressive array of Abe artifacts, including his trademark top hat, and its period décor and old-time demonstrations shine a light back to an earlier era. Guided tours of the 24-room mansion are offered daily at noon, though the self-guided version should be sufficient for most.

Be sure to leave yourself ample time to linger on the

second floor, as the house's upper-level windows frame bird's eye views of the surrounding mountains.

Indeed, for all its history-steeped interiors, the best of Hildene is outdoors. Set on 412 pristine acres, Hildene's grounds include refined gardens, farmland and trail-crossed woodlands. Configured in the pattern of a stained glass window, the formal gardens offer spectacular mountain and valley views alongside thousands of flowering plants, which reach their peak in June with the onset of peony season. Trails are as well suited to summer walks as snowshoeing excursions. If you're short on time or simply more into nature than history, purchase a grounds pass to save money while still exploring the estate to your heart's content.

ALTERNATIVE PLAN

More the outdoor type? The Manchester area offers easy access to the southern part of "Skiers' Row" along Route 100. **Bromley** and **Stratton** resorts are mere minutes from town and ideal for a day excursion or special ski weekend. Fewer crowds and relatively tame terrain make Bromley one of Vermont's best family-centered mountain experiences, while Stratton is the better choice for snowboarders and those looking for a "bigger" experience. Both resorts offer recreation opportunities in warm weather too, from **Bromley's Alpine slide** – the longest in North America – to **Stratton's trio of nine-hole golf courses.** Chairlift and **gondola rides** are also a great way to experience the autumn foliage. *Info*: *Bromley Mountain Ski Resort, 3984 Route 11, Peru. Tel. 802-824-5522. www.bromley.com. Stratton Mountain Resort, off Route 30, Bondville. Tel. 800-787-2886. www.stratton.com.*

Info: 1005 Hildene Rd
Open daily 9:30 am-4:30 pm
Tel. 802-362-1788
www.hildene.org
Admission $12.50, $5 for
grounds only

The rest of your southwest Vermont weekend is all about **Bennington**. This historic town in the state's southwestern corner has all the ingredients for a pleasantly full final day. From the Bennington Monument to Bennington Potters, our one-day plan above has you covered for history, artistry, gastronomy and more.

A WEEK IN SOUTHWESTERN VERMONT

With the advantage of extra time, you can see both Bennington and Manchester more in depth while also acquainting yourself with the best of the surrounding towns and trails. You could easily hike, ski or shop a week away here, so your interests will largely determine how you spend your additional time.

For example, you can shop till you drop and then do it again the next day in **Manchester Center**. One mile north of Manchester Village via Route 7A, this one-time factory hub turned consumerist paradise features hundreds of premier brands in upscale outlet settings. Whether you're couture-conscious or cost-conscious, chances are you'll emerge from the "Fifth Avenue of the Mountains" with a bag or two. **Manchester Designer Outlets** is among Manchester Center's prime shopping destinations,

though it's not *all* boutiques and box stores. Even the most jaded anti-consumerist is bound to appreciate **Northshire Books** – widely considered Vermont's best bookstore – and its sister Spiral Press Café.

Info: Manchester Designer Outlets
97 Depot St/Route 7A

*Open Mon.-Sat. 10 am-6 pm,
Sun. 10 am-5 pm
Tel. 800-955-7467
www.manchesterdesigneroutlets.com*
Northshire Books
*4869 Main St
Open Sun.-Thurs. 10 am-6
pm, Fri.-Sat. 10am-9pm
Tel. 802-362-2200
www.northshire.com*

Manchester's shopping-plus-nature aesthetic makes it a natural fit as headquarters for **Orvis**, the outdoor equipment and apparel company that was founded here in 1856. The flagship store on Route 7A stocks thousands of rods and reels and offers a range of fly fishing classes on the Battenkill River. Anglers will also appreciate the easy access to the **American Museum of Fly Fishing** next door.

Info: *Orvis*
4104 Main St. at Route 7A

*Open Mon.-Fri. 9am-6pm,
Sun. 10am-5pm
Tel. 802-362-3300
www.orvis.com.*
*American Museum of Fly Fishing
Open Tues.-Sat. 10am-4pm
www.amff.com
Admission $10*

Shopping meets the outdoors *and* the arts at the **Southern Vermont Arts Center**, a 400-acre multipurpose estate and art complex west of Manchester Center. Listed on the National Register of Historic Places, its sprawling grounds on the slope of Mt. Equinox encompass a sculpture garden, trails, a concert hall and a pair of first-rate exhibition spaces. The mansion-size **Wilson Museum** houses the Center's permanent collection of 19th and 20th century art while the Yester House mansion houses 10 galleries popu-

SIGHTS

lated with contemporary work for sale.

Info: 2522 West Rd
Open Tues.-Sat. 10am-5pm,
Sun. 12-5pm
Tel. 802-362-1405
www.svac.org
Admission $8

The allure of such attractions aside, you'd certainly be forgiven for forsaking civilization altogether for a week in the great outdoors. The **Appalachian Trail** passes just east of Manchester, and the hiking in and around the **Green Mountain National Forest** is among Vermont's best.

The **Burr Burton Trail** makes an amazing ascent up **Mt. Equinox**, the highest peak in the Taconic Range. A strenuous five-hour trek from town to the summit, it's strictly for experienced hikers, though beginner and intermediate trails around the mountain's base offer a panoramic taste of that which lies above. Other great outdoor options are scattered throughout the countryside, from the scenic **White Rocks National Recreation Area** southeast of Wallingford to the **Delaware and Hudson Rail-Trail**, a biking hub a half-

hour northwest of Manchester Center via Routes 30, 315 and 153.

A number of small but no less scenic villages populate the surrounding countryside. Continuing six miles northwest from Manchester on Route 30 brings you to **Dorset**, another model New England town defined by its village green, marble sidewalks and clapboard homes. A study in whitewashed, green-shuttered civility, it's among the most exceedingly pleasant stops on the Vermont time machine.

The **Dorset Inn**, the state's oldest continually operating inn, is the standard bearer among an elite crop of lodging options, while the **Dorset Playhouse** is a classic destination for top-notch summer theater. Dorset's not all refinement, though. A range of peaks – Owl's Head, Dorset Mountain – rise up around it, and its roads lead to some of the state's most gorgeous driving territory, particularly north of town along Route 30 to 315, where the climb up Rupert Mountain affords vistas of pristine green hills and farmland.

Info: Dorset Inn
8 Church St. at Route 30
Tel. 802-867-5500
www.dorsetinn.com
Dorset Playhouse
104 Cheney Rd
Tel. 802-867-5777
www.dorsetplayers.org.

Ten miles from Manchester and 15 miles from Bennington, small-town **Arlington** is worth a look for its covered bridges, high-class inns and **Norman Rockwell Museum**. Bridge enthusiasts will want to seek out the **Chiselville Bridge** on East Arlington Street and the Battenkill River-spanning **West Arlington Bridge** (*see photo below*). On the oppo-site side of Route 7A off Route 313, the latter is among Vermont's most photogenic.

Housed in a converted Gothic church, the **Rockwell Museum** pays homage to the *Saturday Evening Post* illustrator and 14-year Arlington resident with a small exhibition of his nostalgia-driven works. It's worth a visit for Rockwell fans but is the most dispensable of the museum options in this section.

Info: Route 7A
Open daily 9am-5pm, May-Oct., 10am-4pm Nov.-April
Tel. 802-375-6423
Admission $4

SIGHTS

More impressive is the **Park McCullough House Museum**, a classic Second Empire Style mansion that's packed to its gilded rafters with an impressive collection of American antiquities. Its finely wrought interiors – all wood paneling and bronze chandeliers – are as grand as the rose-gardened grounds. The ten minute trip there from downtown Bennington's not without its charms either – it follows the **Walloomsac River** past a trio of covered bridges.

Info: 1 Park St., N. Bennington
Open daily 10am-4pm mid-May-Oct
Tel. 802-442-5441
www.parkmccullough.org
Admission $8

Vermont's #1 literary landmark, the **Robert Frost Stone House Museum**, is also just outside Bennington, four miles to the north in Shaftsbury. America's most beloved poet lived in this quaint, colonial-style home for nearly a decade and composed "Stopping by Woods on a Snowy Evening" here in 1922. Today the stone and timber house museum and its surrounding land are like a Frost poem come to life, its

seven acres studded with stone walls, apple trees and other signature Frost imagery.

Info: 121 Rte 7A
Open Tues.-Sun. 10am-5pm May-Dec
Tel. 802-447-6200
Admission $4

For more history mixed with artistry, visit the **Bennington Center for the Arts** in town. Part gallery, part engineering exhibition, its assets include locally produced landscape paintings and portraits (many for sale) and the small but engaging Covered Bridge Museum. The latter's interactive exhibits shed light on the bridges' construction and function and even help you plan an impromptu bridge tour.

Info: 44 Gypsy Ln. at Route 9
Open Wed.-Mon. 10am-5pm
Tel. 802-442-7158
benningtoncenterforthearts.org
Admission $9

Among Bennington County's five covered bridges, the closest is the Silk Covered Bridge almost immediately opposite Bennington College. The campus of this small yet elite private school is pleasant to stroll too, its modernist buildings and emphasis on the experimental underscoring the liberal in the liberal arts.

Bennington's best spots for connecting with nature include **Woodford State Park** (a 400-acre tract surrounding the Adams Reservoir 10 miles east of town on Route 9) and the **Battenkill River**, a canoeing hotbed that runs down from Arlington. The **Long Trail** also passes through the area, and Mt. Snow is less than an hour to the east.

A trip to southwest Vermont can also be easily combined with excursions to Lenox and Williamstown, Massachusetts; Saratoga Springs, New York; and the Berkshires – worthy destinations all just minutes from Bennington but outside the jurisdiction of this book.

BEST SLEEPS & EATS

BENNINGTON
Four Chimneys Inn $$$

Next to the Old Governor's Mansion and Old First Church, this sprawling white house with, yes, four chimneys is the only bed and breakfast in Old Bennington. It doubles as one of the area's top restaurants and serves a hearty country breakfast in the sunroom or main dining room. Guest rooms are well

appointed – some have marble baths, fireplaces and views of Mt. Anthony – while the separate Ice House suite affords additional space and privacy. *Info: www.fourchimneys.com. Tel. 802-447-3500. 21 West Rd. 11 rooms.*

Alexandra B&B $$

With views of the mountains and the Bennington Monument, this 1859 farmhouse is a small gem set on two acres on the edge of town. The innkeepers are accommodating, and the spacious,

spotless guest rooms offer amenities such as gas fireplaces and water jet tubs. The intimate on-premises bistro is open to guests only and serves a four-course candlelit dinner by reservation. *Info: www.alexandrainn.com. Tel. 802-442-5619. 916 Orchard Rd. 12 rooms.*

Henry House $$

The former home of a Revolutionary War hero, Henry House dates to 1769 and is registered as a national historic site. Six working fireplaces lend warmth to sparse yet nicely-decorated guest rooms that look out on to a covered bridge, the Walloomsac River and 25 acres of pinelands and meadows. *Info: www.henryhouseinn.com. Tel. 802-442-7045. 1338 Murphy Rd., N. Bennington. 6 rooms.*

Paradise Inn $-$$

A ten minute walk from the town center, the Paradise may not quite live up to its name, but it remains one of southern Vermont's finest upper-tier motels. Rooms, though dated, are a good size and attractively furnished, and the property includes a heated outdoor pool, gazebo, tennis courts and a small garden. The north building offers the best access to the grounds, and a small café is on the premises. *Info: www.theparadisemotorinn.com. Tel. 802-442-8351. 141 Main St. 77 rooms.*

Knotty Pine Motel $

This family-owned, pet-friendly motel is conveniently situated between downtown and Bennington College. Its clean budget rooms and efficiency suites have acquired a loyal following that's based on value and the welcoming and knowledgeable staff. *Info: www.knottypinemotel.com. Tel. 802-442-54877. 130 Northside Dr. 21 rooms.*

Pangaea $$-$$$
Bennington's finest, locally focused dining room also features an inviting outdoor terrace and a tavern serving lighter fare. The "precontinental" cuisine ranges from seared half chicken to Thai curry, and the wine list has made *Wine Spectator's* best since 2003. Powers Market across the street serves breakfast and lunch and is under the same ownership. *Info: 1 Prospect St., N. Bennington. Tel. 802-442-7171. Dinner Tues.-Sat. www.vermontfinedining.com.*

Bennington Station $$-$$$
Bennington's restored train station is both a historic landmark and the site of this chef-owned restaurant known for its lengthy menu and superb salad bar. Ranging from surf and turf style specialities to "monumental" 3/4 pound burgers and pastas, the menu employs train themes and also offers numerous options for children. *Info: 150 Depot St. Tel. 802- 442-7900. Lunch and dinner daily. www.benningtonstation.com.*

Alldays and Onions $$
Named after an obscure British auto manufacturer, Alldays and Onions has driven Bennington's casual dining scene for over 20 years. Tasty and efficient by day – deli-style lunch options include custom sandwiches (veggie burgers, hot pastrami on rye) and salads – it also serves bona fide sit down dinners Thursday through Saturday and wholesome morning meals on weekends. *Info: 519 Main St. Tel. 802-447-0043. Breakfast Sat., brunch Sun., lunch Mon.-Sat., dinner Thurs-Sat. www.alldaysandonions.com.*

Rattlesnake Café $$
Oversized chimichanga and sizzling fajitas are highlights at this casual Mexican cantina that's also one of Bennington's better watering holes. Vegetarian entrees and novel dishes such as Aztec shrimp and steak roja give the menu nearly as much variety as the margarita list. *Info: 230 North St. Tel. 802-447-7018. Dinner daily. www.rattlesnakecafe.com.*

Blue Benn Diner $
No trip to Bennington is complete without a meal in this classic 1945 dining car. Whether in one of the half-dozen booths or on

stools at the counter, hungry diners pack in tight here for homestyle breakfasts and blue plate specials. The homemade donuts, omelettes, whole wheat pancakes and melt-in-your-mouth meatloaf are all justly famous. Expect a wait on weekends. *Info: 318 North St. Tel. 802-442-5140. Breakfast and lunch daily, dinner Wed.-Fri.*

MANCHESTER
The Equinox $$$

The standard by which all New England resorts are judged, the Equinox has been a Manchester landmark since 1769. Blessed

with a picture perfect setting – the village green directly in front, the rise of Mount Equinox behind it – this historic AAA Four Diamond property is looking better than ever after a recent multimillion dollar facelift. The redesigned Great Room feels soothing yet exclusive, as do the custom beds and soft modern décor of the guest rooms. Deluxe rooms in the main inn are large and well-appointed and are just one of many desirable choices on the property. Luxury suite options, townhomes and country inn style accommodations (at the 1811 House and Charles Orvis Inn) offer something for every preference. With four on-site restaurants and a stunning range of activities – from a spa (complete with beautiful indoor pool) and top-rated golf course to falconry, fly fishing and off-road driving schools – entertainment and dining options are just as extensive. *Info: www.equinoxhotel.com. Tel. 800-362-4747. 3567 Main St. 183 rooms.*

Reluctant Panther Inn $$$

This small, all-suites inn in downtown Manchester's among Vermont's most chic boutiques. Four-poster feather beds, fireplaces and hydrotherapy spa tubs are standard luxuries that can be made even more romantic with add-ons like in-room roses and champagne. The main inn contains 11 rooms, with the remaining nine in the smaller but equally luxurious carriage, porter and garden houses. The grounds look out onto Mount Equinox and include a small bridge-spanned pond and fountain. A full breakfast is included, and you'll wish dinner was too, as the Panther's fine dining is among the best (and most expensive) in the area. *Info: www.reluctantpanther.com. Tel. 802-362-2568. 17-39 West Rd. 20 rooms.*

Inn at Manchester $$-$$$
Classy country is the theme of the Inn at Manchester, a classic 19th century white house set among four acres of lawns and gardens. Guest rooms are appointed with antique wood furniture, brass beds and handmade quilts and range from the soothing Lavender room to the large, newly renovated Sage suite with vaulted ceiling and private balcony. Upstairs rooms are more spacious but also, in some cases, more staid. A high quality art collection, an on-premises pub and an ample country breakfast are among the inn's other comforts. *Info: www.innatmanchester.com. 3967 Main St. Tel. 800-273-1793. 18 rooms.*

Barnstead Inn $$
A 19th century hay barn turned inn, the Barnstead offers comfortably rustic accommodations just two blocks from the town center. Rooms are classically decorated and have beautiful exposed wood beams. All have private baths, some have fire-

places and the grounds include a pond, a pool, a small garden and a barbecue pit. *Info: www.barnsteadinn.com. Tel. 800-331-1619. 349 Bonnett St. 17 rooms.*

Seth Warner Inn $$
From the library to the dining room to the red-walled sitting room, cozy common areas distinguish this small, colonial-style inn. The quaint charm extends into the guest rooms, which feature exposed beams, hand-stenciled wall trim and canopied

beds with country quilts, and throughout wooded grounds that are seeded with gardens, a brook and a duck pond. *Info: www.sethwarnerinn.com. Tel. 802-362-3820. 2353 Main St. 5 rooms.*

The Equinox $$$

With four excellent in-house options (five if you count the golf course's Dormy Grill), the Equinox's dining facilities are as extensive as its range of accommodations. The **Chop House** steak palace is the most extravagant choice. Its cuts are as generous as the large wooden tables, and the atmosphere is enhanced by the space's original Orvis stone hearth. The **Marsh Tavern** is welcoming for lunch and dinner and serves a pub menu alongside classic New England fare. The elegant **Colonnade** dining room is the place for breakfast, and the **Falcon Bar** provides a rich lounge experience whether you snack on cheese and chocolates in the leather and dark wood-described interior or relax with a drink on the fire pit-enhanced outdoor deck. *Info: 3567 Main St. Tel. 800-362-4747. Breakfast, lunch and dinner daily. www.equinoxresort.com.*

Mistral's at Toll Gate $$$

Tucked off in the woods, this secluded and intimate French bistro is one of Manchester's most romantic dining experiences. Re-

quest a table with a view of the spotlighted stream outside, then treat your other senses to exquisite gourmet fare (salmon, duck, filet mignon) and a wine list that has earned *Wine Spectator's* Award of Excellence for the past 15 years. *Info: 10 Toll Gate Rd. Tel. 802-362-1779. Dinner Thurs.-Mon., Thurs.-Tues. July-Oct.*

Perfect Wife Restaurant & Tavern $$-$$$

This atmospheric dining room and more casual tavern make a great partnership. Dine on specialties such as sesame-crusted yellowfin tuna in the stonewalled main restaurant and garden room or on more humble fare such as meat loaf and the famous "couch potatoes" in the fireplaced pub. Live music is often offered in the tavern on weekends. *Info: 2594 Depot St. Tel. 802-362-2817. Dinner Mon.-Sat. Reservations recommended. www.perfectwife.com.*

Ye Olde Tavern $$
Dating to 1790, this colonial-style restaurant serves classic American fare (turkey, pot roast, cranberry fritters) in a candlelit dining room made all the cozier with antique hardwood furniture and a fireplace. The three-course early bird special (until 6 pm every day but Saturday) is a superior value. *Info: 5183 Main St. Tel. 802-362-0611. Dinner daily. www.yeoldetavern.net.*

Laney's Restaurant $$
Laney's recently celebrated 20 years of home style cooking. The open kitchen has a wood-fired oven that produces wonderful homemade breads and pizzas, and the selection of barbecued meats, sides and wings is equally enticing. *Info: 1716 Depot St. Tel. 802-362-4456. Dinner daily. www.laneysrestaurant.com.*

Candeleros $$
This train stop-turned-cantina has a colorful southwest style and a relatively authentic menu of south of the border favorites such as fajitas, burritos and chile rellenos. Order them with a house margarita or tequila sampler for an extra kick. *Info: 5103 Main St. Tel. 802-362-0836. Lunch and dinner daily. www.candeleros.net.*

Little Rooster Café $
Manchester's best breakfast is served out of a charming little wooden house with awnings and a dozen tables. Daily specials, omelettes and the Rooster's famous hash are favorites with locals and tourists alike, and there's little doubt they're worth the wait that's inevitable here at peak times. *Info: 46 Pleasant St. Tel. 802-362-3496. Breakfast and lunch daily.*

SLEEPS & EATS

SLEEPS & EATS

DORSET

The Dorset Inn $$$

Vermont's oldest continually operated inn is also one of its most charming. Set right on the village green, it's welcomed guests for

well over two centuries and, with the addition of a day spa, a fine dining room and other modern amenities, it's only gotten more luxurious in recent years. A stately columned exterior speaks to the well-preserved interiors and period furnishings within, which include elegant wall patterns and handmade wood furniture. Upper floor guest rooms afford views of the village green, and suites up the ante with spacious sitting areas, flat screen televisions and baths with heated marble floors and whirlpool tubs. A full breakfast is included, and dinner is served in the formal dining room and more casual tavern. Pets are not only permitted but welcomed with their own beds and water bowl. *Info: www.dorsetinn.com. Tel. 802-867-5500. 8 Church St. at Route 30. 25 rooms.*

Inn at Westview Farm $$

Originally a working dairy farm, this 1870s farmhouse has been an inn now for nearly a century. The old fashioned guest rooms are decorated with country antiques and come with private baths, mountain views and access to the inn's restaurant, which serves an excellent breakfast (that's included) as well as dinner Thursday through Monday – reservations are recommended. *Info: www.innatwestviewfarm.com. Tel. 802-867-5715. 2928 Route 30. 10 rooms.*

Chantecleer $$$

A renovated dairy barn in East Dorset conceals one of Vermont's most intimate and gourmet dining experiences. Charming as much for its ambiance (nooks, stone fireplace) as its French provincial cuisine, Chantecleer specializes in seafood (whole dover sole, house escargots), game and homemade desserts and is completely worthy of a splurge. The three-course menu deal makes a meal here surprisingly attainable – provided you can resist the call of the masterful wine list. *Info: Route 7A, E. Dorset. Tel. 802-362-1616. Dinner Wed.-Sun. Closed in winter. www.chantecleerrestaurant.com.*

Dorset Inn $$$
Elegant Comfort Food is the title of this 200 year old inn's cookbook, and it might well serve as the kitchen's motto too. Local, organic ingredients are front and center in the selection of artisan cheeses and entrees such as coq au vin and beer braised brisket from Boyden Farms. A four-course chef's tasting menu is also available by pre-order. As you'd expect from one of the region's premier inns, breakfast is a gourmet meal unto itself with fresh squeezed juices, homemade hash and multiple varieties of pancakes. Dine in the casual fireplaced tavern or in the inn's formal red dining room (though jeans are banned in the latter). *Info: 8 Church St. at Route 30. Tel. 802-867-5500. Breakfast, lunch and dinner daily. www.dorsetinn.com.*

ARLINGTON
West Mountain Inn $$$
Surrounded by gardens, trails and mountain views, Arlington's classiest farmhouse inn feels at once rustic and Victorian. Whether you prefer the lacy Lincoln room or the pine-paneled Booker T. Washington, you'll feel at home amongst the house's nooks, fireplaces and porches. An adjacent cottage and converted mill  each contain three additional rooms. Breakfast is included; a deluxe five-course dinner is available by reservation in the inn's wood-paneled dining room. *Info: www.westmountaininn.com. River Rd. Tel. 802-375-6516. 20 rooms.*

SLEEPS & EATS

STRATTON-BROMLEY AREA

Stratton Mountain Resort $-$$$

From the luxurious **Long Trail House** (*photo below*) to the affordable **Liftline Lodge**, Stratton offers a wide variety of overnight accommodations. The Long Trail's modern, condo-style lodging is the best option if you can afford it; the extra investment

nets you access to the heated parking garage, a trio of outdoor hot tubs and an inviting common area with leather couches and a fireplace. If you'd rather put that money towards lift tickets, though, the Liftline is a reasonable budget choice. Rooms are spartan and service limited but within easy walking distance of the lifts and the village. *Info: Stratton Mountain Rd. off Route 30, Bondville. Tel. 800-787-2886. www.stratton.com.*

Bromley View Inn $$

Friendly innkeepers and three even more sociable Labrador retrievers greet you at this excellent little inn known for its hearty breakfasts and wide mountain views. Guest rooms are bright and clean, if basic, and common areas include a deck and lounge area with pool table. Suite-style accommodations are also available. *Info: www.bromleyviewinn.com. 522 Route 30, Bondville. Tel. 877-633-0308. 17 rooms.*

Bromley Sun Lodge $

Bromley Mountain's only slopeside hotel offers basic accommodations but an ultra-convenient location at reasonable rates. Parts of the hotel have been recently renovated, and amenities include a very small and (somewhat!) heated indoor pool, fitness center, nice common room with fireplace, and on-site bar and restaurant. Mountainside rooms have balconies with views of the slopes while those on the valley side look out onto the Green

Mountain National Forest. *Info: www.bromleysunlodge.com. Tel. 800-722-2159. 4216 Route 11, Peru. 51 rooms.*

Verde $$$
This high-end Mediterranean grill is Stratton's best dining experience. Locally raised ribeye and Colorado lamb noisette stand out on a meat-centered menu that also includes pastas, salads and gourmet sides. Lunch is served weekends and includes gourmet fare such as grilled king salmon and a ferocious venison burger. *Info: Stratton Courtyard, Landmark Building. Tel. 802-297-9200. Lunch Sat.-Sun., dinner Wed.-Mon. www.stratton.com.*

Johnny Seesaw's $$
Built by a Russian logger in the twenties, this rustic lodge-style inn at the foot of Bromley Mountain offers large portions and lively atmosphere in its hearth-encircling dining room. Three cuts of prime rib and the special duck cassis highlight the French chef's menu of traditional favorites. *Info: 3574 Route 11, Peru. Tel. 802-824-5533. Dinner daily. www.jseesaw.com.*

Mulligan's at Stratton $$
An Irish pub in the middle of the mountains, this Stratton Village favorite serves burgers, sandwiches, steaks and nightly specials and has a bar with a lengthy beer list and nightly après-ski specials. In addition to Mulligan's, the resort village is also home to a number of other casual dining establishments, including the Mulberry Street Ristorante and the Copper Cup coffeeshop. *Info: Stratton Village Square. Tel. 802-297-9293. Lunch and dinner daily. www.stratton.com.*

SLEEPS & EATS

BEST SHOPPING

Bennington

Lined with galleries and mom-and-pop shops, **Main Street** makes for a lovely small-town shopping experience. Bookworms will want to peruse the **Bennington Bookshop's** wide-ranging stock, and it's hard to walk past the **Village Chocolate Shop** without stopping to visit Benny, the 82-pound chocolate moose.

Bennington Potters (*324 County St., Tel. 800-205-8033*), in Old Bennington, is also a must-browse. Its factory and outlet store are filled with artisan-made mugs, plates and bowls that make distinctive, functional gifts. For more ideas and activities in the area, visit the town's Web site, *www.bennington.com*.

Manchester

Outlets – more than 100 in all – rule the Manchester Center shopping scene. You'll find Armani, Ann Taylor and other top names in fashion at **Manchester Designer Outlets** (*97 Depot St., Tel. 802-362-3736*), and the **Battenkill and Highridge Outlets** on Route 7A (*Tel. 802-362-5272*) are prime destinations for designer fashions and mainstream goods alike.

For outdoor apparel, the **Orvis** flagship store (*also on Route 7A, Tel. 802-362-3750*) stocks the best clothing and equipment – including thousands of fishing rods and reels – from its famous catalog. Manchester Center also has its share of small, independent shops, from **Millstone Antiques** (*4478 Main St.*) to **Northshire Books** (*4869 Main St.*), and Manchester Village offers some good shopping as well, particularly the **Village Shops** across the green from the Equinox Hotel. For more information visit *www.manchestervermont.net.*

The villages around Manchester provide a more old-fashioned shopping experience. General stores, antique shops and galleries prevail in **Dorset** and, to a lesser extent, **Arling-** ton. Jewelry, quilts and custom furniture can all be found in and around town, and you can buy just about anything at the converted barn-occupying **H.N. Williams** department store on Route 30 in Dorset. For more suggestions in Dorset visit *www.dorsetvt.com.*

BEST NIGHTLIFE & ENTERTAINMENT

Bennington

Plasma-screen televisions and house brews make the **Madison Brewing Company** (*428 Main St., Tel. 802-442-7397*) Bennington's best late night stop. A full pub menu and the vats-and-vintage-beer-can décor make it worth an earlier visit as well. Bennington's performing arts scene offers evening entertainment as well; check the **Oldcastle Theatre Company's** schedule at the **Bennington Center for the Arts** (*44 Gypsy Ln., Tel. 802-447-0564*) or the range of events at **Bennington College** (*www.bennington.edu*).

Manchester

The Equinox Hotel's **Falcon Bar** (*3567 Main St., Tel. 800-362-4747*) is Manchester's most plush late night hang-out, and many other top inns and restaurants have equally appealing bars and lounges. The **Spiral Press Café** (*at Northshire Books, 4869 Main St., Tel. 802-362-2200*) is open late on weekends and makes a nice spot for reading or low-key conversation. Arts-related options include the summer concert series on the village green; the historic **Village Picture Show** movie theater in Manchester Center (*263 Depot St, Tel. 802-362-4771*); and the **Dorset Players** (*104 Cheney Rd., Tel. 802-867-5777*), one of the top theater companies in the region.

Among the area's resorts, the après-ski scene at Stratton is the most robust. **Grizzly's**, in the main base area, and the **Green Door Pub** at Mulligan's

(Tel. 802-297-0171) offer drink specials and live entertainment, and the **Domaine Wine Bar** in Stratton Village

(*Tel. 802-437-2977*) serves finer beverages till 9 pm Thursday through Monday.

BEST SPORTS & RECREATION

Bennington

On Route 9 ten miles east of Bennington, **Woodford State Park** offers 398 acres of high-elevation terrain as well as access to lakes, ponds and the trails circling the Adams Reservoir. The **Long** and **Appalachian Trails** also pass through the area, and **Glastenbury Mountain** offers beautifully remote hiking trails with appeal to beginners and experts alike. **Prospect Mountain** on Route 9 is the best destination for cross-country skiing.

River tours are another popular pursuit outside Bennington. **BattenKill Canoe** (*Tel. 800-421-5268, www.battenkill.com*) offers rentals and tours that let you float or paddle past the region's mountains, woods and meadows. If you're looking for even more leisurely pursuits, you can hit the links at Bennington's **Mount Anthony Country Club** (*180 Country Club Dr., Tel. 802-442-2617*). The 18-hole public course was recently renovated and has become one of the area's best.

ASK A RANGER!

Not sure which outdoor adventure's the one for you? Then visit the **Green Mountain District Ranger Station** in Manchester. It dispenses free literature with details on nearly 20 area trails. *Info: Route 11 & 30 (east of Route 7). Tel. 802-362-2307.*

Manchester

The Appalachian Trail passes just east of Manchester, and the hiking in and around the Green Mountain National

FULL MOON SNOWSHOEING AT STRATTON

Among Stratton's more novel winter activities are its **Saturday evening snowshoe hikes**. They happen on select moonlit nights (roughly one per month) and depart at 6 pm from the Stratton golf course parking lot. Reservations are required. *Info: Tel. 802-297-4230.*

Forest is among Vermont's best. The **White Rocks National Recreation Area** southeast of Wallingford is part of both, and the trails leading through woods and past **Chaos Canyon** – a cleft in a huge quartzite rockslide – place it among the area's most intriguing outdoor destinations.

Once a railroad track serving the slate industry, the **Delaware and Hudson Rail-Trail** offers some of the state's best mountain biking. Half an hour northwest of Manchester Center, with end points in West Rupert and Castleton, it runs in two 10-mile sections through forest and farmland, over a number of bridges and past the occasional industrial relic.

Manchester's signature peak, **Mount Equinox**, is its most accessible outdoor experience. Veteran hikers will want to follow the **Burr Burton Trail** to the top (a five-hour trek from town to summit), and there are also beginner and intermediate trails skirting the mountain's base.

In the shadow of the mountain, the **Equinox Resort** (*www.equinoxresort.com*) offers a range of luxury outdoor experiences. In addition to a fly fishing school and Top 75 golf course (as ranked by *Golf Digest*), it's home to truly unique facilities such as the British School of Falconry and the Land Rover off-road driving school.

Bromley and Stratton resorts are both nearby and offer countless outdoor options in all seasons. Six miles east of Manchester, **Bromley** is one of the oldest continuously-running ski areas in the country. Its 43 trails are serviced by 10 lifts and are primarily of the beginner and intermediate varieties. The more advanced skiing is on the mountain's east side, and there are snowboarding facilities as well. The **Bromley Thrill Zone**, with miniature golf, an alpine slide and new cable coaster, makes the resort a popular family destination in summer. For more information visit *www.bromley.com*.

Stratton is the area's biggest outdoor resort experience. Twice the size of Bromley and with more than twice as many trails, it offers runs for every skill level and top-notch terrain parks (including an 18-foot superpipe) that have long made it number one with snowboarders. Three nine-hole golf courses, a tennis school and a range of extreme sports make it a year-round destination as well. Even if you're not the sporting type, the views from the gondola make Stratton worth the 15-mile drive from Manchester. For more information visit *www.stratton.com*.

5. WOODSTOCK & THE UPPER CONNECTICUT RIVER VALLEY

HIGHLIGHTS

▲ Woodstock

▲ Quechee/Simon Pearce

▲ Billings Farm & Museum

▲ Plymouth Corner & Windsor

▲ Okemo/Suicide Six skiing, hiking

INTRO

If the name **Woodstock** brings to mind images of cartoon birds and hippie farmland, it won't once you visit Vermont's signature village. Full of boutiques, inns and historic attractions, this Woodstock is a genteel paradise that's been a top tourist destination for centuries. The combination of colonial character, first-class amenities and nearby attractions like **Quechee Gorge** make the area a playground for visitors in all seasons.

COORDINATES

Woodstock and **Quechee** are located along Rt. 4, accessible from I-89 or I-91. To get to **Plymouth Corner**, take Rt. 100A south from Rt. 4 for six miles. **Windsor** and **Mt. Ascutney** are south of Woodstock on Rt. 44.

WOODSTOCK SIGHTS IN A DAY

The local Chamber of Commerce humbly calls **Woodstock** the "prettiest small town in America," and after just one day in town you're bound to agree. This quintessential New England village offers timeless beauty alongside great shopping and some of the best lodging and dining in Vermont.

The town of Woodstock dates back to 1761, and the influence of leading American families like the Rockefellers has kept the town rich in history and decorum ever since. Impressively preserved and impossibly gentrified, every brick and blade of grass seems in its proper place. Nary a power line disturbs Woodstock's old time essence – the city's forefathers had the foresight to lay them underground.

Woodstock's most scenic location is no doubt its **village green**. Among Vermont's most eminently photographable spots,

SIGHTS

SIGHTS

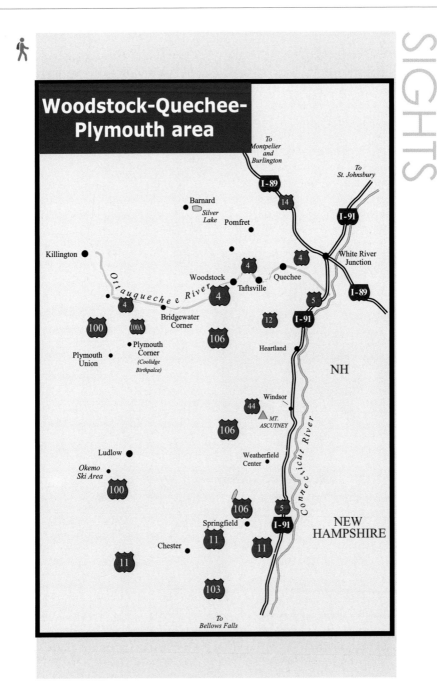

Woodstock-Quechee-Plymouth area

SIGHTS

the green is an iconic New England scene, its long oval lawn flanked by Georgian & Federal style buildings, a covered bridge and one of the most celebrated inns in Vermont. Along with the handsome brick courthouse, the **Woodstock Inn** anchors the green's south side while the **Middle Bridge**, Vermont's most visited covered bridge,

extends from the north side over the **Ottauquechee River** and forms the gateway to residential Woodstock.

Take a moment to appreciate the green's timeless beauty, then make your way east into Woodstock's charming **consumer district**. Lined with shops and quaint street lamps,

Central and **Elm Streets** are the main thoroughfares, and they intersect at the eastern end of the green, Elm leading north and Central leading east. As befitting its history as a playground of the landed gentry, much of Woodstock's shopping is of the high end variety. Its boutiques and art and antique dealers are ideal for seeking out that special purchase (or window shopping).

There are a number of down to earth destinations here too, from the **Yankee Bookshop**, the state's oldest continually operating independent bookseller, to the **F.H. Gillingham & Sons** general store, a National Historic Landmark that sells pretty much everything under the sun. Just up the street from the general store, the **First Congregational Church** is another centuries-old landmark. It dates to 1808, and the bell on the front porch was made by Paul Revere.

Info: *Yankee Bookshop*
12 Central St
Tel. 802-457-2411
www.yankeebookshop.com
F. H. Gillingham & Sons
16 Elm St
Tel. 800-344-6668

SIGHTS

www.gillinghams.com
First Congregational Church
36 Elm St
Tel. 802-457-9818
www.fccw.net

Elm Street continues out of the village center as Route 12 and leads to the **Marsh-Billings-Rockefeller National Historical Park**. Vermont's only national park is just a half-mile from the green, and an afternoon here in any season is the perfect complement to a morning spent in town. From its hilltop mansion overlooking Elm and River Streets to the acres of preserved forest around it, the park contains wonders inside and out.

Home to early conservationists George Perkins Marsh and Frederick Billings and later owned by the Rockefellers, the historic three-story mansion was built in the Queen Anne Style with ornate brickwork, tall chimneys and a wide porch. **Guided tours** are offered on the hour and lead through chambers full of original furnishings and personal treasures from railroad memorabilia to landscape paintings. Interior exhibitions impart lessons of land stewardship and conservation that are under-scored by the beauty of the surrounding outdoors.

Gardens rise up around the mansion and then give way to less formalized open space. Stone walls and covered bridges dot the landscape, and twenty miles of trails snake through 550 acres of preserved forest full of centuries-old spruce, beech and sugar maple. This is some of the oldest forestland in the country, and it's ideal for hiking and cross country skiing.

A highlight is the trek through the **Mount Tom Forest** with its 14-acre pond known as "The Pogue" near the summit. South Peak also makes for a simple and super pleasant stroll. More hill than mountain, it starts from the Faulkner Path on Mountain Avenue and

SIGHTS

overlooks the town and the surrounding Ottauquechee Valley.

Info: 54 Elm St
Visitors' center open daily 10am-5pm. House and garden tours available late May-Oct
Tours $8
Tel. 802-457-3368
www.nps.gov/mab

Before night falls, make your descent back into town and avail yourself of Woodstock's array of **fine dining**. From candlelit gourmet to classic country, a memorable meal awaits you: an elegant *prix fixe* spread at the Prince & the Pauper or classic bistro fare at Bentley's. **Pentangle Arts** on the green is Woodstock's prime option for evening entertainment. It offers exposure to all sides of the arts, from first run movies to concerts and children's theater.

Info: Prince & the Pauper
24 Elm St
Tel. 802-457-1818
Bentley's
3 Elm St
Tel. 802-457-3232
Pentangle Arts
31 The Green
Tel. 802-457-3981
www.pentanglearts.org.

A WEEKEND IN THE WOODSTOCK AREA

A weekend in Woodstock offers the opportunity for an extended stay at a classic inn or bed and breakfast as well as increased exposure to the historic attractions around town. Spend Friday night and Saturday in Woodstock, then take a day trip down to **Quechee** on Sunday to see its gorgeous gorge and historic village center.

Start the weekend off right with a special lodging experience. Many establishments

offer complimentary wine and cheese or evening tea that will set you right at ease after a long trip. Kick back in a cozy sitting room, socialize if you see fit and perhaps, if you're staying in town, take an **evening stroll through historic Woodstock**. Whether blanketed in autumn color, snow or summertime glow, the village green and town center possess a romantic allure that lingers long after the sun has set.

Come Saturday, you can pretty much follow the Woodstock one-day plan above, adding another historic attraction or two according to your time and interest. The **Billings Farm & Museum** is the top option for anyone looking for an authentic glimpse into rural Vermont life. Adjacent to the Marsh-Billings-Rockefeller National Historical Park, this fully-functioning farm has been in operation since the 1860s and celebrates the area's rural heritage with an array of interactive programs and demonstrations. The restored farmhouse contains a creamery complete with butter churning and ice cream making demonstrations, and the outer grounds

are domain to all sorts of animals, including sheep, oxen and chickens. Plan to visit in the afternoon, as the Jersey cows are milked daily at 3:15 pm.

Info: Route 12 and River Rd
Open daily 10am-5pm May-Oct., weekends 10 am-4 pm Nov.-Feb
Admission $11
Tel. 802-457-2355
www.billingsfarm.org.

For a more craft-centric glimpse into the past, visit the Woodstock Historical Society's **Dana House Museum**. Founded in 1807, it brings past centuries back into focus with a treasure trove of early Americana that includes antique furniture, silver, ceramics and textiles. Among the most fascinating are an exhibit of colonial era toys and the collection of old photographs that provide a sepia-

SIGHTS

SIGHTS

tinged glimpse into how Woodstock developed.

Info: *26 Elm St*
Open Wed.-Sun. 11am-4pm
June-Oct
Tel. 802-457-1822
Admission $5
www.woodstockhistorical.org

Start your Sunday with **brunch at the Woodstock Inn** and some additional time in town or around the historical park and museum. Plan to depart Woodstock around noon for Quechee. The five-minute drive down Route 4 leads through Taftsville and past the picturesque **Taftsville Covered Bridge**, the third oldest covered bridge in Vermont.

Info: *Woodstock Inn*
14 The Green
Tel. 802-457-1100

Upon reaching **Quechee Village**, you'll be charmed immediately by the approach into town, which involves crossing another covered bridge – this one set below a waterfall. Quechee means "swift mountain stream" in the local Native American dialect, and the rushing river below, the **Ottauquechee**, is

pretty much responsible for the town's existence (to say nothing of its charm). Not only did it supply the power for the town's nascent industries, but it singlehandedly carved out Quechee Gorge, one of the most striking natural wonders in all of Vermont.

The small yet historic village center that awaits you on the other side of the river features a handful of shops along Main Street, but its most distinguished structure is the beautiful old mill that's the headquarters of the **Simon Pearce glassblowing company and store**. Idyllically overhanging the river, this combination glass factory, restaurant and store is a cultural, culinary and shopping attraction all in one.

SIGHTS

Here you can observe master glassblowers and ceramic artisans at work; learn about hydroelectric power; and enjoy a gourmet meal with a river view, a waterfall and a covered bridge just on the other side of the window. Make a reservation at the restaurant beforehand, and if you like the tableware as much as the meal, hit the Simon Pearce retail store on the way out. You'll find museum-grade pieces, high quality functional items and some great bargains among the factory seconds.

Info: 1760 Main St
Open daily 10am-9pm
Tel. 802-295-2711
www.simonpearce.com

Enjoy a late lunch at Simon Pearce, then proceed on to beautiful, inspiring **Quechee Gorge** by mid-afternoon. Just a few miles east of the village center, "Vermont's Grand Canyon" cuts a narrow, tree-lined swath 163 feet down to the riverbed and is the centerpiece of the 600+ acre **Quechee Gorge State Park**. Its hiking trails are easily navigable and accessed from the gift shop/ welcome center. One of the most popular hikes in Vermont, the leisurely, mile-long **Gorge Trail** leads through red pine forest, past a dam and Dewey's Mill Pond to the **waterfall** at the head of the gorge. This is the best way to connect with the canyon up close, though the most photogenic vantage is from the Route 4 highway bridge overlooking the gorge.

Info: 764 Dewey Mills Rd
Trails open mid May-Oct
Tel. 802-295-2990

SIGHTS

ALTERNATIVE PLAN

While it may sound dire, the **Suicide Six** ski area is among the area's best outdoor destinations for families. Manageable with just 23 trails spread over 100 acres, it's operated by the **Woodstock Inn** and dovetails nicely with a weekend stay there. Golf, tennis and horseback riding options make the Inn's outdoor packages a great option in warmer weather too. *Info*: *14 The Green, Tel. 802-457-6661, www.woodstockinn.com.*

Some of Vermont's biggest outdoor resorts are just around the corner from Woodstock too. Versatile **Okemo** (*photo above*), in particular, offers something for the entire family, from award-winning children's programs to skiing, golf, tennis and spa services. *Info*: *77 Okemo Ridge Rd., Ludlow, Tel. 802-228-4041, www.okemo.com.*

A WEEK IN THE UPPER CONNECTICUT RIVER VALLEY

For a wonderful week in and around Woodstock, split your time between town and the periphery. From farmstands to trails, there's plenty to do within a few minutes' drive, and Windsor, Weston and the towns to the south offer an even wider range of activities.

A great little ride outside town is the six-mile jaunt along Route 4 and Hillside Road that leads through a covered bridge to the **Sugarbush Farm**. Livestock roam Sugarbush's hillside pastures, and the farm takes intense pride in its array of cheeses and maple syrups. Learn how both are made and sample 14 varieties of cheddar and four grades of syrup while you're at it.

Info: *591 Sugarbush Farm Rd*
Open Mon.-Fri. 8am-5pm,
Sat.-Sun. 9am-5pm
Admission free
Tel. 802-457-1757
www.sugarbushfarm.com

The **Vermont Institute of Natural Science** is a nature center of another kind. One-and-a-half miles from the Woodstock Green, it's a fiefdom for feathered friends with trails and outdoor exhibits on more than 25 different birds of prey. The raptor center and songbird aviary are standout segments. A stop here is great in tandem with a visit to Quechee Gorge, as the trails here connect with those of adjacent Quechee State Park.

Info: *6565 Woodstock Rd.*
Open daily 10am-5pm May-Oct; Wed.-Sun. 10am-4pm Nov.-April
Admission $9, children $7
Tel. 802-359-5000
www.vinsweb.org

Heading southeast from Woodstock or Quechee leads first to the natural paradise

WOODSTOCK HISTORIC SITE COMBO TICKET

If you plan to visit both the **Billings Farm and Museum** and the **Marsh-Billings-Rockefeller National Historical Park**, you can save money by purchasing a combination ticket. Joint admission tickets are valid for two days, allowing you ample time to see both. Note: only valid from Memorial Day through Oct. 31. *Info*: www.billingsfarm.org/visit/index.html

that is North Hartland Lake and then further south to **Windsor**, home of the **Harpoon Brewery**. The largest craft brewery in New England, Harpoon (which also brews in Boston) makes 55,000 barrels of IPA, UFO Hefeweizen, and more here annually, and the Windsor location features a production viewing area and a lunchtime beer garden. Serious beer geeks should plan to visit Friday or Saturday for an in-depth brewery tour (3pm both days).

Info: *336 Ruth Carney Dr, Windsor*
Open Sun.-Wed. 10am-6pm,

SIGHTS

SIGHTS

Thurs.-Sat. 10am-9pm (closed Mon. in winter)
Tel. 888-427-7666
www.harpoonbrewery.com

Aside from some 19th century churches and Victorian houses, Windsor itself isn't much to look at, though it does boast the **longest covered bridge in the world** – the **Cornish-Windsor Bridge** – spanning the Connecticut River to New Hampshire. Windsor is also the cornerstone of the **Precision Valley** – so named for its status as an early hotbed of industrial design.

You can explore this side of the area's heritage at the **American Precision Museum**. Housed in a 160-year old former armory building, this National Historic Landmark features an array of Industrial Revolution era products and the most extensive collection of historic machine tools in the country, from sewing machines to typewriters to firearms.

Info: 196 Main St
Open daily 10am-5pm late May-Oct
Admission $6
Tel. 802-674-5781
www.americanprecision.org

On Route 44 West only four miles from Windsor, **Mount Ascutney** rises up to provide panoramic Green Mountain views and high quality hiking and skiing. Roam any of Mount Ascutney State Park's four trails (located on the mountain's northeast face); drive up the toll road to the summit; or settle in at Ascutney Mountain Resort for summer or slopeside recreation. The resort itself is in transition and far from luxurious, but the mountain provides a scenic setting and some of the best terrain around.

Info: Mt. Ascutney State Park
1826 Back Mountain Rd. off Route 44A, Windsor
Open mid May-mid Oct
Tel. 802-674-2060
Ascutney Mountain Resort
Route 44, Brownsville
Tel. 802-484-7000
www.ascutney.com

Just north of Windsor Route 91 passes through and will take you north to White River Junction and **Norwich**. The former is a rather faceless transit hub, but Norwich is a lovely little town that's home to the Norwich Inn and the Montshire Natural History

SIGHTS

Museum. There's some fantastic **backroad driving** to be had in the entire greater Woodstock area (*see photo at right*). From Norwich you can take Route 132 northwest up to Sharon and return to Woodstock via the scenic Pomfret Road south.

Info: Norwich Inn
325 Main St
Tel. 802-649-1143
www.norwichinn.com
Montshire Natural History Museum
1 Montshire Rd. off Route 10A
Open daily 10am-5pm
Admission $9
Tel. 802-649-2200
www.montshire.org

Southwest of Woodstock, Route 4 leads past the **Old Mill Marketplace** – a historic shopping complex with local artisan shops, an antique center and the largest ski warehouse in Vermont – and the Lincoln Covered Bridge to Bridgewater Corners, a small town best known as the base of the **Long Trail Brewing Company**. Vermont's #1 craft brewer has a riverside pub and visitors' center that's modeled after Munich's

Hofbrau House, and it makes an inspired stop for an early meal or a pint of its top-selling Double Bag Ale.

Info: Long Trail Brewing Company
Junction of Routes 4 and 100A
Open daily 10am-6pm
Tel. 802-672-5011
www.longtrail.com

Following Route 100A south at this junction leads to **Plymouth**. Just six miles from Woodstock, it's best known as the birthplace of **Calvin**

SIGHTS

Coolidge, and both a historic site and state park here are named after him. The Coolidge Historic Site features a dozen exhibits, including the family homestead (fully restored to its 1923 condition), a general store, the cheese factory established by Coolidge's father and a fascinating tool and carriage filled barn.

*Info: 3780 Route 100A
Open daily 9:30am-5:30pm
late May-mid Oct
Admission $7.50
Tel. 802-672-3773
www.historicvermont.org/
coolidge*

The Calvin Coolidge State Park is part of the huge (21,500 acre) **Coolidge State Forest**, the largest public landhold-

COVERED BRIDGE HEAVEN!

Vermont is home to **106 covered bridges** that are distributed broadly throughout the state. Pictured below is the **Lincoln Covered Bridge** near Woodstock. The longest is the **Windsor-Cornish Covered Bridge**, which – at 465 feet – is the longest two-span covered bridge in the world. For everything you ever wanted to know about covered bridges, visit Virtual Vermont, which includes a complete list of the state's bridges sorted by county, town and bridge name. *Info: www.virtualvermont.com/ coveredbridge.*

ing in Vermont. Its trails feature technicolor views of the Green Mountains and the Black River. Take the scenic hike up **Slack Hill** on the park's eastern edge.

Info: 855 Coolidge State Park Rd. off Route 100A
Open late May-Oct
Tel. 802-672-3612

Traveling much beyond Plymouth or Bridgewater Corners brings you to Route 100, which leads north to **Killington** and south to **Ludlow**, home to one very small village and one very large resort (**Okemo**). Continuing beyond Ludlow on Route 100 will bring you to Weston – home of the **Weston Playhouse** summer theater and the legendary, wood-planked **Vermont Country Store** – or you can split off onto Route 103, which leads to **Chester**, a small yet impressive village with two historic districts and a surprising cache of Victorian buildings.

Info: Weston Playhouse
703 Main St
Tel. 802-824-5288
www.westonplayhouse.org
Vermont Country Store
657 Main St
Open daily 9am-5:30pm
Tel. 802-824-3184.
www.vermontcountrystore.com

This entire area is fertile territory for backroad exploring and pretense-free country lodging. See also the chapters on southeast Vermont and the Killington region.

SLEEPS & EATS

BEST SLEEPS & EATS

WOODSTOCK
Jackson House Inn $$$

A landscaped English garden, a pond and acres of meadow surround this elegant, yellow Queen Anne style house that's on  the National Register of Historic Places and just one mile outside the center of town. Built in 1890 as a private residence, the house itself is full of period details, including stained glass, artisanal woodwork and floors of oak, cherry, maple and pine. Guest rooms have classic French décor and are individually appointed with ornate four-poster beds, silk wall coverings and French doors. They have so much character you may never want to leave them, but if you do, there are plenty of other spots to relax in this AAA Four Diamond Inn, from the library to the sauna to the award-winning dining room to a rocking chair on the front porch. *Info: www.jacksonhouse.com. Tel. 802-457-2065. 114-3 Senior Ln. 13 rooms. No kids under 16.*

Woodstock Inn & Resort $$$

Laurance S. Rockefeller founded this classic resort inn that's among the most historic and luxurious in Vermont. The stately white mansion has peerless ambiance, with the village green for a front yard and a stunning fieldstone hearth in its main foyer. Many rooms have working fireplaces along with beautiful hardwood furniture, Thistle bath products and chocolates at turn down. Blending the best attributes of a country inn with the amenities of a re-  sort, the property also boasts three restaurants, a 41,000 square foot racquet and fitness club, indoor and outdoor pools and access to hiking trails, skiing (at Suicide Six) and the Robert Trent Jones-designed Woodstock Golf Course. *Info: www.woodstockinn.com. Tel. 802-457-1100. 14 The Green. 142 rooms.*

Hawk Inn & Mountain Resort $$$

A 70-acre bird and wildlife sanctuary is at the center of this country retreat in the heart of the Green Mountains. Stables, an apple orchard, a fly fishing school and miles of trails are all spread over the 1,200-acre Plymouth property that would be a must-visit even without the luxurious resort accommodations. Private two to four bedroom mountain villas with decks and fieldstone fireplaces are as beautiful as they are exclusive, and premier guest rooms are decorated with designer furnishings, sleigh beds and Simon Pearce lamps. Even standard rooms come with Vermont marble baths and bay windows that look out over the Black River. A library, indoor and outdoor pools and a full service spa with redwood sauna complete a lodging experience at once extravagant and off the beaten path. *Info: www.hawkresort.com. Tel. 800-685-4295. Rte. 100, Plymouth. 50 rooms.*

Deer Brook Inn $$

This 1820 farmhouse on five acres is both a nice inn and a great value for Woodstock. All rooms have hardwood floors and come with private baths, river or mountain views and a three-course candlelit breakfast. Room 4 has a gorgeous pine sleigh bed while the spacious Schubert suite features a sitting room and canopied bed. *Info: deerbrookinn.com. 535 Woodstock Rd. Tel. 802-672-3713. 5 rooms.*

SLEEPS & EATS

Kedron Valley Inn $$

Featured annually in Budweiser's holiday commercials, the Kedron Valley is one of Vermont's oldest inns. Under new ownership in 2008, its best features are its private lake access (complete with white sand beach) and homey rooms with four-poster beds, exposed wood beam ceilings and wide pine floors. Many rooms have a fireplace or woodburning stove. Most are in the red-bricked main house, with a handful contained in the Tavern and Log Lodge buildings. *Info: www.kedronvalleyinn.com. Tel. 800-836-1193. Route 106, S. Woodstock. 37 rooms.*

Woodstocker Inn $$

The fresh coat of yellow paint on this 1830s farmhouse symbolizes the traditional yet brightly modern comforts within. Guest rooms have both flat screens and fresh flowers and a contemporary yet rustic feel with great woods, bright colors and baths with stone tile floors and claw foot tubs. The Chester Room is a good value while the Richmond three room suite is all luxury with a private deck, leather seating and a Bose media center. Other strengths include a great library, the attentions of Stanley the Wheaton terrier and an inn-wide organic emphasis that extends beyond breakfast to the duvets and soaps. *Info: www.woodstockervt.com. Tel. 802-457-3896. 61 River St. 9 rooms.*

Grist Mill House $

Just south of the village, this 230-year-old mill has been transformed into a small treasure of an inn with fantastic rates and country ambiance. The building itself is on the National Historic Register, and its large hand-hewn beams, old doors and floors lend great rustic character. Woven baskets hang from the ceiling of the common area, which boasts a wood stove, rocking chairs and a leather couch. The humble yet charming guest rooms have handmade quilts and antique beds and share a single bathroom with a slate floor and tub. *Info: www.gristmillhouse.com. Route 106, S. Woodstock. Tel. 802-457-3326. 3 rooms.*

Jackson House Inn $$$

Warmth emanates from this elegant dining room's granite hearth all the way up to its beamed cathedral ceiling, and its rustic yet formal atmosphere is mirrored in a modern New England cuisine that's focused on local produce, game and cheeses. Lobster, duck and organic pork entrees are fixtures of the five course *prix fixe* menu, and if you have

difficulty deciding between them, the only solution is to pull out all the stops and order the deluxe tasting menu with wine pairings. The Jackson House's extensive wine list routinely wins *Wine Spectator's* Award of Excellence. *Info: 114-3 Senior Ln. Tel. 802-457-2065. www.jacksonhouse.com. Restaurant is seasonal; check for days and hours.*

Barnard Inn $$$

The three-course *prix fixe* menu changes seasonally at this wonderful little restaurant eight miles north of Woodstock in Barnard. A 300-year-old brick building houses both the fireplaced main dining room and the more informal Max's Tavern. Both are popular with locals and serve unassumingly spectacular fare from soups to schnitzel to seafood. *Info: 5518 Route 12, Barnard. Tel. 802-234-9961. Dinner Tues.-Sat. (tavern) and Thurs.-Sun (main dining room). www.barnardinnrestaurant.com.*

The Prince & the Pauper $$-$$$

Eat like a king at this elegant yet informal restaurant next to the Dana House Museum. *Prix fixe* and bistro menus feature specialties like veal scallopine and rack of lamb and the wine list has received *Wine Spectator's* Award of Excellence. For food, ambi-

SLEEPS & EATS

ance and service, dollar for dollar, there's no better dining experience in Woodstock. *Info: 24 Elm St. Tel. 802-457-1818. Dinner daily. www.princeandpauper.com.*

Osteria Pane e Salute $$-$$$

Food and Wine has lauded this intimate, upscale Italian eatery and wine bar as one of its 50 most amazing wine experiences. Pair a flight of its rare vintages with the four-course *prix fixe* menu or a classic thin-crust pizza. *Info: 61 Central St. Tel. 802-457-4882. Dinner Thurs.-Sun. Closed April and Nov. www.osteriapaneesalute.com.*

Bentley's $$

Dark and dramatically decorated with antique lamps and couches, Bentley's provides superior ambiance alongside decent pub fare, salads and custom brewed ales. As both bar and dining room, it's been a Woodstock institution for over 30 years. *Info: 3 Elm St. Tel. 802-457-3232. Lunch and dinner daily, Sun. brunch. www.bentleysrestaurant.com.*

Long Trail Brewery $-$$

Vermont's number one selling craft brewery serves pub fare alongside its lineup of local beers at its visitors' center and pub at the junction of Routes 4 and 100A. Drink and dine beside the warming wood stove in winter or on the riverside patio in summer, and take a self-guided brewery tour before or after. *Info: Routes 4 and 100A, Bridgewater Corners. Tel. 802-672-5011. Open daily 11 am-5 pm. www.longtrail.com.*

Mountain Creamery $

Savor homemade ice cream while looking out onto the Woodstock street scene from the front of this longtime town favorite. Also known for its heaping sandwiches and apple pies, the ever-popular creamery often draws lines for its old-fashioned booths and cones to go. *Info: 33 Central St. Tel. 802-457-1715. Open daily.*

QUECHEE
Parker House Inn $$-$$$

Renovated in recent years, this large, red brick Victorian contains seven bright and airy guest rooms and one of the best little bistros in the area. Third floor rooms – particularly the spacious Victoria – are a great value while the more luxurious Joseph room comes with river views and a Jacuzzi tub. A full breakfast is served on the porch in summer and in the dining room in winter. *Info: www.theparkerhouseinn.com. 1792 Main St. Tel. 802-295-6077. 7 rooms.*

Simon Pearce $$$

The glassblowing factory's falls-overlooking restaurant is one of central Vermont's essential dining experiences. Equal parts rustic and romantic, its old mill setting and covered bridge views would make it a serious destination even without the gourmet menu, superior service and signature Simon Pearce glassware. Dinner here is a worthy indulgence while lunch offers similar ambiance at wallet-friendly prices. *Info: 1760 Main St. Tel. 802-295-1470. Lunch and dinner daily, Sun. brunch. www.simonpearce.com.*

Parker House Bistro $$

French Gothic architecture and nightly farmers' market specials highlight the dining component at Quechee's most romantic bistro. Candlelit ambiance, a stocked wine cellar and fresh seafood (particularly the mussels of the day) all add up to a superlative inn-style dining experience. *Info: 1792 Main St. Tel. 802-295-6077. Dinner daily. www.theparkerhouseinn.com.*

Farmer's Diner $

Part in a restored dining car and part in an old barn, this classic diner's all day breakfasts and lunches are made primarily with local and organic ingredients. As described in Barbara Kingsolver's *Animal, Vegetable, Mineral*, it's been a big part of Vermont's "localvore" movement. Menu highlights include omelets served

SLEEPS & EATS

with house-baked English muffins and the Sticky Hen roast chicken sandwich that comes slathered with maple-infused barbecue sauce. *Info: 5573 Route 4. Tel. 802-295-4600. Breakfast and lunch daily. www.farmersdiner.com.*

OKEMO/LUDLOW
Okemo Mountain Lodge $$$

In the middle of the resort near the Clock Tower, Okemo Mountain Lodge's one-bedroom "residences" are mini-suites with outdoor decks, breakfast bars and standard hotel furnishings. Easy access to the resort's lifts, restaurant and Spring House fitness and aquatic center furthers their appeal. If you're looking

for additional space and amenities, Okemo also offers a number of on-site inn and condo options, some of which are ski-in, ski-out. The new Bixby House in Jackson Gore Village offers large, luxuriously low-key accommodations while the condos at Solitude Village come with stone fireplaces, sun decks and proximity to the new Epic restaurant. *Info: www.okemo.com. Tel. 800-786-5366. Okemo Ridge Rd. 76 rooms (main lodge).*

Inn at Weathersfield $$-$$$

Set on 21 wooded acres ten miles from Okemo, the Weathersfield combines the amenities of a boutique hotel with the charm of a country inn. Treat yourself to a massage in the therapy room, dine in the inn's classy tavern, or simply retire to one of the pleasantly quaint guest rooms. The second floor Hammond Room has exposed beams and a four-poster pencil bed while a spiral staircase leads to the deluxe Martins Mill room with whirlpool and roof deck. The parlor also invites relaxation with a fireplace and afternoon refreshments. *Info: www.weathersfieldinn.com. Tel. 802-263-9217. 1342 Route 106, Perkinsville. 12 rooms.*

Echo Lake Inn $$

Just five minutes from Okemo, the Echo Lake Inn first opened in 1840 as a summer hotel. Antique bureaus and brass beds lend its 23 guest rooms an old-fashioned flair, though some have Jacuzzi tubs and other modern luxuries. Tennis courts, a swimming pool and hot tub are among the inn's other outdoor amenities, and a lakefront dock provides canoes, rowboats and beautiful waterside views. *Info: www.echolakeinn.com. Tel. 800-356-6844. Route 100, Tyson. 23 rooms.*

Okemo Mountain Resort $-$$$

On-mountain dining options at Okemo include Sitting Bull at the main base lodge and the Coleman Brook Tavern at the Jackson Gore Base Lodge. The former offers pub fare and live music on weekends while the latter is more gourmet and serves traditional New England cuisine alongside an award-winning wine list. The new Epic dining room at Solitude Village is quickly gaining a reputation for its innovative lunch menu that includes duck quesadillas and swordfish with Japanese eggplant. *Info: Okemo Ridge Rd. Tel. 800-786-5366. www.okemo.com.*

Inn at Weathersfield $$-$$$

The chef at this prize Ludlow inn won last year's Vermont Chef of the Year. Choose from tasting menu and à la carte options in the more formal Fireside Dining Room or opt for the lighter, casual menu at Lucy's Tavern. Both offer exceptional ambiance and service, nightly specials and an extensive drink list. *Info: 1342 Route 106, Perkinsville. Tel. 802-263-9217. Dinner Wed.- Sun. www.weathersfieldinn.com.*

Cappucino's $$

Pasta specials, a range of meats (veal, strip steak, fresh half duck) and homemade desserts distinguish this Ludlow village favorite. As you might expect from the name, they pull a mean espresso, and the wine list has won *Wine Spectator's* Award of Excellence six years running. *Info: 41 Depot St., Ludlow. Tel. 802-228-7566. Dinner daily. www.cappucinosrestaurant.com.*

SLEEPS & EATS

SLEEPS & EATS

Harry's Café $$

With weekly Thai nights and a killer Jamaican jerk sauce to go with its menu of regional favorites, Harry's has gained a reputation as Vermont's "general store of ethnic eating."Chef-owned, it's just five miles north of Okemo and has a sister location, Little Harry's, in downtown Rutland. *Info: Route 103, Mt. Holly. Tel. 802-259-2996. Dinner Wed.-Sun. www.harryscafe.com.*

WINDSOR
Windsor Station Pub $$

Whether you've just disembarked from the Vermonter or have come from the slopes of Ascutney, you'll feel refreshed after a meal and a pint in Windsor's century-old train station. Under new direction as of 2008, the kitchen serves everything from burgers to steaks to butternut gnocchi and nods to its past with transporting flourishes such as onion rings served around a rail spike. *Info: 27 Depot St. Tel. 802-674-2052. Dinner daily. www.windsorstation.com.*

BEST SHOPPING

SHOPPING

Woodstock
Downtown Woodstock is a quaint shopper's paradise full of galleries, boutiques and gift shops. Central and Elm streets are lined with street lamps and one-of-a-kind stores, including the artisan-owned **Collective Gallery** (*47 Central St.*); the **Aubergine** gourmet kitchen store (*1 Elm St.*); and **Krystyna's** (*20 Central St.*), a silver jeweler with unique goods imported from Mexico. The **F.H. Gillingham & Sons** general store (*16 Elm St.*) is a National Historic Landmark, and the

Yankee Bookshop (*12 Central St.*) is one of the state's oldest independent booksellers.

Just one mile west of town, the **Woodstock Farmers' Market** (468 Woodstock Rd.) offers the region's best food products, including gourmet gift items to go. It operates six days a week (closed Monday), and the local atmosphere is a delight. Further west of the village in Bridgewater Corners, the **Old Mill Marketplace** on Route 4 is a top stop for its antique center, ski warehouse and range of local crafters. The **Shackleton Thomas** store's collection of handmade furniture and pottery is top of the line, and you can see demonstrations while you shop. The **Simon Pearce** glassblowing factory in Quechee (*1760 Main St.*) also offers museum-grade housewares alongside artisan demonstrations. The old mill ambiance makes shopping here a joy, and even the factory seconds of its glassware and ceramics are exquisite.

Quechee

Quechee offers a handful of other shopping opportunities, including the Quechee Gorge Village shopping area, which features an antique mall and craft center, a gift shop and an outpost of the **Cabot cheese company** (*5573 Woodstock Rd.*). For all-purpose shopping with a focus on Vermont products, visit the **Taftsville Country Store** on Route 4 between Woodstock and Quechee or make the drive south to Weston, where you'll find the legendary, wood-planked **Vermont Country Store** (*657 Main St.*), one of the biggest – and best – in the state.

For more information on shopping in and around Woodstock, visit *www.woodstockvt.com.*

THE VERMONT COUNTRY STORE

In business for over 60 years, the Vermont Country Store is among the state's most fabled family-owned stores. With a stock of antiques, oddities, essentials, classic candies and more, the original red, porch-fronted location in Weston is a pleasure to

browse, and the "new" (as of 1967) location in Rockingham makes a convenient stop just off I-91. *Info: 657 Main Street, Weston and 1292 Rockingham Road, Rockingham. Tel. 802-362-8460. www.vermontcountrystore.com.*

NIGHTLIFE & ENTERTAINMENT

BEST NIGHTLIFE & ENTERTAINMENT

Though genteel Woodstock tucks in early, many restaurants and inns have their own lounges and bars in which you can while away the evening hours. The dark Victorian bar at **Bentley's** (*3 Elm St., Tel. 802-457-3232*) is the most inviting one in town. If you prefer your beer directly from the source, two of Vermont's largest microbreweries – **Long Trail** in Bridgewater Corners (*5520 Route 4, Tel. 802-672-5011*) and **Harpoon** in Windsor (*336 Ruth Carney Dr., Tel. 888-427-7666*) – are a short ride away. Both have appealing brewpubs, though they maintain relatively modest hours.

For performing arts in Woodstock, **Pentangle Arts** (*31 The Green, Tel. 802-457-3981*) presents a regular schedule of concerts, plays and first-run movies at the historic Town Hall Theatre on the village green.

BEST SPORTS & RECREATION

From the back woods to the back nine, Woodstock's sporting pursuits come in many styles. You can play a round of championship-quality golf at the Robert Trent Jones-designed **Woodstock Country Club** (Tel. 802-457-6674); do a little skiing at **Suicide Six** (*photo at right; Tel. 802-457-6661*); or even take a scenic hot air balloon ride with **Balloons Over New England** (*Tel. 800-788-5562*). Many inns offer outdoor packages that bundle lodging and dining with golf, tennis, horseback riding and more.

Hiking enthusiasts will enjoy the gently sloping trails of Mount Tom. Within the **Marsh-Billings-Rockefeller National Historical Park's**

SPORTS & RECREATION

550 acres, they lead through old-growth forest and past the 14-acre pond known as the "Pogue" on their way to the summit. The **South Peak trail**, which starts from the Faulkner Path on Mounain Avenue, also makes a pleasant stroll. Serious hikers can also pick up the **Long Trail** in Bridgewater just a few miles west of Woodstock.

Mere minutes from Woodstock in the other direction, **Quechee Gorge** (*photo below*) is the area's most popular hiking destination. The mile-long Gorge Trail is the most well-traveled section of the 600-acre **Quechee Gorge State Park** (*off Route 4, Tel. 802-295-2990*), for good reason. It's scenic and navigable, and the waterfalls at the head of the gorge are truly spectacular. For a more off-the-beaten path gorge experience, start out on the Vermont Institute of Natural Sciences' adja-cent trails just west of the gorge or follow North Hartland Lake to the gorge's mouth. **Wilderness Trails** (*Tel. 802-295-7620*) helps with canoe, kayak and bike rentals and also runs a fly fishing school on local streams.

South of Windsor, good hiking and skiing can also be found at **Ascutney State Park** (*off Route 44A, Tel. 802-674-2060*) and **Ascutney Mountain Resort** (*off I-91, www.ascutney.com*). **Okemo Mountain Resort** in Ludlow (*off Route 103, www.okemo.com*) is the area's premier big-mountain experience. Its 632 acres of terrain are most popular with skiers. The mountain has 119 trails, five terrain parks and the **largest vertical drop in southern Vermont** – and a pair of 18-hole golf courses (Okemo Valley and Tater Hill) – plus tennis, swimming and fitness facilities for year-round fun.

6. KILLINGTON & THE MAD RIVER VALLEY

HIGHLIGHTS

▲ **Killington/skiing & hiking**

▲ **Middlebury**

▲ **Rutland**

▲ **Waitsfield & Warren/Lake Champlain**

▲ **Morgan Horse Farm**

INTRO

The Upper Green Mountains are all about the outdoors. **Killington**, the "Beast of the East," is the largest ski resort in the area and a year-round recreational paradise. The **Green Mountain National Forest** and

the **Mad River Valley** are among the state's foremost natural treasures with off the beaten path options for hiking, biking, skiing and more. **Lake Champlain** laps against the region's northwest edge, and there are even a handful of notable gateway towns here too, from blue-collar **Rutland** to literary **Middlebury**.

KILLINGTON SIGHTS IN A DAY

Ski resorts don't come any bigger than **Killington** (*photo on previous page*). The supersized mountain complex encompasses Vermont's second highest peak – and six other neighboring mountains too. Often thrilling, occasionally overwhelming and always expensive, Killington's an all-around exercise in excess – and one ski and extreme sport enthusiasts owe it to themselves to experience first hand.

Famous as the largest ski resort in eastern North America, Killington is actually much more than that. Think of it rather as a **four-season moun-** tain playground that also features championship golf, award-winning adventure sport parks, spectacular spa services and dazzling fine dining and nightlife. In visiting for a day, your primary challenge will be to choose an activity or two and then return to the real world.

In winter, **skiing and snowboarding** are obviously the primary pursuits. Killington's slopeside superlatives include **the largest snowmaking system in North America**; a greater vertical drop than any other New England mountain; and the high-

SIGHTS

SIGHTS

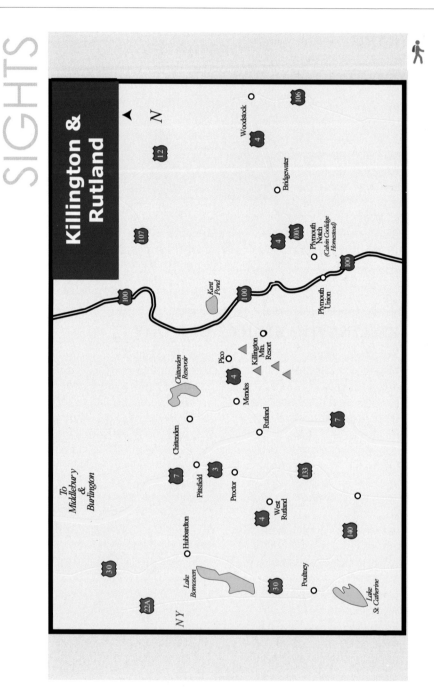

Killington & Rutland

est lift-served terrain in Vermont. You'll traverse but a few of its **200 trails** in one day, so choose wisely. Standout tracks include the lengthy Juggernaut; the even keeled Cruise Control; and the double black diamond Big Dipper Glade. If you're visiting Killington during prime time, consider forgoing some of the more popular, widely cut trails on the main mountain for the more secluded but no less scenic runs on adjacent **Pico Peak**.

Killington also boasts six challenging **freestyle parks**, including the all-new, all-natural Stash terrain park and Outer Limits, one of the steepest mogul runs in New England. The **superpipe on Bear Mountain** is perhaps the resort's second most impressive technical accomplishment – behind only the efficiency of the lifts. Need some guidance? Seek out a Snowshed ski ambassador. They lead free mountain tours daily and can come in very handy!

When the snow thaws and Killington Peak turns back to green, an even more dizzying array of outdoor options appears. From gondola rides to alpine slides, you name it, Killington has it. **Mountain bikers** can spin their wheels over 45 + miles of steep terrain in the **Kona Park** (and can even access the trails via lift). There's **fabulous hiking** to be had all over, particularly on **Deer Leap Mountain**. The adventure center on Pico Mountain has something for the entire family, from the alpine slide to mini-golf to a climbing wall, and there are even more leisurely activities elsewhere on the resort. Take a guided horseback ride through woods and meadows or kick your legs through cool mountain air from the **Killington Gondola** as you drink in views of five states and Canada.

The one thing that Killington lacks is a town center. There's an assemblage of restaurants, hotels and bars along Killington Road and Route 4, but otherwise visitors are reliant on the resort for food and entertainment. Fortunately its fine dining and nightlife options are up to the challenge. Conclude your day with a gourmet meal at **Ovations** at the Killington Grand or extend it later into the night at a hot après-ski spot like **Mahogany Ridge**.

Info: *Killington Resort
4763 Killington Rd
Tel. 802-422-6200 or 800-621-6867 for reservations
www.killington.com*

A WEEKEND IN THE KILLINGTON AREA

There's so much to do at the resort that you really need a weekend to get the full Killington experience. Whether you're here for skiing, golf or the legendary nightlife, take advantage of Killington's range of packages for an incredibly luxurious multi day getaway.

If you know what you like, a stellar Killington weekend is basically the day plan above times two. You're here, so go ahead – ski the mountains or hit the links all weekend long. Weekend lift tickets shave a bit off day rates while packages such as ski and spa specials combine separate pursuits with significant savings. Advance online purchase (*www.killington.com*) locks in the best deals.

The majority of weekend packages are built around **lodging**, and their combination of convenience and savings makes them worth examining. With not one, not two, but seven lodges on site, it can be overwhelming just deciding where to stay. The king of the hill is the **Killington Grand Resort and Spa**. It recently received a $2.5 million makeover and

has the best location right on the mountain and steps from the golf course. Everything from the slopes to the spa is pretty much at your fingertips here. Another favorite, the **Highridge Condominiums**, offers more deluxe accommodations a mile from the slopes while the Mountain Inn is popular with young people for its energetic nightlife. Both connect easily to the mountain via shuttle. If you need assistance in choosing, Killington Central Reservations represents hundreds of lodging options throughout the region, from hotels and inns to condos and rental homes. If you're not that particular, avail yourself of the resort's "Snow Blind" deal and save a bundle on whatever lodging happens to be available.

Info: *Killington Resort*
4763 Killington Rd
Tel. 802-422-6200 or 800-621-6867 for reservations
www.killington.com

Another advantage to staying in Killington is increased access to its **nightlife**. Hands down the liveliest of any Vermont resort, the late night scene here goes until all hours and caters to the young, glamorous and single. Somewhere between a cruise ship and a college campus on a Friday night, there's a distinct party vibe throughout the resort that extends from après-ski spots like **Bear Mountain Lounge** to the bars and dance venues along **Killington Road**.

Some may shy away from such indulgence, and for many Killington is not without its faults. Some call it "K-Mart" for its impersonality, and as with most megacomplexes, what you gain in options and efficiency you sacrifice in

SIGHTS

charm. It can be way too big for those used to more intimate resorts, and the crowds, the costs and the youth-driven party scene may also conspire against you. There's no arguing the size, strength and diversity of Killington's amenities, but for a lower-key experience and a closer sense of Vermont, you're more likely to enjoy Stowe, Sugarbush or Mad River Glen.

ALTERNATIVE PLAN

For an entirely different mountain experience, head north to Mad River Glen, a cooperatively-run ski area that harkens back to the way Vermont skiing used to be. Its iconic single chair lift has been in operation for 60 years; there's little to no snowmaking; and

snowboarding is expressly prohibited. Depending on your perspective, it's either hopelessly outmoded or the greatest thing ever.

As for the skiing – well, there's no debating that. Nearly half of Mad River Glen's slopes are classified as expert, and the mountain's motto – "Ski it if you can" – makes its challenge implicit. *Info: Route 17, Waitsfield. Tel. 802-496-3551. www.madriverglen.com.*

SIGHTS

A WEEK IN KILLINGTON, RUTLAND, MIDDLEBURY & THE MAD RIVER AREA

I certainly wouldn't fault you for booking an entire week at one of the outdoor resorts. If you crave time on the trails or on the slopes or are seeking some simple R&R, just do it and read no further. However, with its central location, the Killington area does make a fine launching point for excursions into the surrounding country. You can go in virtually any direction and find more natural wonders alongside historic attractions and other points of interest. To see them all, plan on taking a couple of day trips from your base and ideally spend a night or two around Middlebury and the Mad River Valley.

Rutland is the nearest town to Killington and another jumping off point to the surrounding area. Tucked between the Green Mountain and Taconic ranges, this one time industrial center – known as "Marble City" on account of its quarrying heritage – is Vermont's second largest city. Though rather sprawling and nondescript, it makes a reasonable stop for budget accommodations and as a solid central base whether you're commuting to the mountain or making forays into the wilder country to the north.

Amid the otherwise drab scene of strip malls and box stores along Route 7, Rutland is endowed with a handful of cultural attractions, including the turreted **Chaffee Center for the Visual Arts** and, every September, the **Vermont State Fair**. The historic section of downtown around Merchants Row has also seen some revitalization recently. The quality shopping here serves as some recompense for what many Vermonters consider to be Rutland's cardinal sin: installing a Wal-Mart in the town center.

Info: *Chaffee Center for the Visual Arts*
16 S. Main St
Open Tues.-Sat. 10am-5pm, Sun. 12-5pm. Closed in winter
Admission free
Tel. 802-775-0356
www.chaffeeartcenter.org

Whether you're staying in Rutland, Killington or points north, peripheral Rutland merits a day excursion for its blend of scenic roads, small

SIGHTS

towns and historic attractions. The 20-mile loop along Routes 3, 4 and 7 leads past a series of covered bridges through Proctor and Pittsford and back to Rutland.

Six miles northwest of Rutland, Proctor is most notable for its **Marble Museum**. A staggering stone archway stands at the entrance to the largest marble exhibit in the world, which includes installations on geological history, a collection of Presidential busts and a gift shop with more marble souvenirs than you can imagine. While in Proctor you may also want to visit **Wilson Castle**, a lavish 19th-century mansion that's also made of marble (and brick) and worth a visit for its ornate interiors and palatial landscaped grounds.

Info: *Vermont Marble Museum*
Off Route 3, Proctor
Open daily 9:30am-5pm mid-May-Oct
Admission $7
Tel. 800-427-1396
www.vermont-marble.com
Wilson Castle
W. Proctor Rd. off Route 4
Open daily 9am-6pm late May-Oct

Admission $9.50
Tel. 802-773-3284
www.wilsoncastle.com

If you're more into maple than marble, head over to neighboring Pittsford and tap into the **New England Maple Museum**. Its murals tell the story of sugaring alongside the most complete collection of maple artifacts in Vermont. The museum is open year-round but is best visited during sugaring season in March and April. The Pittsford area also boasts significant outdoor attractions, from hiking on the **Long Trail** to boating on the Chittenden Reservoir, and nearby covered bridges include the Gorham (on Route 3 on the Pittsford-Proctor line) and the Hammond (a mile north of Pittsford off Route 7).

Info: *New England Maple Museum*
Route 7, Pittsford
Open daily 8:30am-5:30pm late May-Oct; 10am-4pm Nov.-Dec., mid March-mid May
Admission $2.50
Tel. 802-483-9414
www.maplemuseum.com

Proceeding northwest from Rutland via Route 7 leads

SIGHTS

through the small town of Brandon and on to Middlebury. If time's not of the essence, branch off at Brandon on to **scenic Route 73**. Whether you travel west and hook up with Route 30 north or drive east over Brandon Gap and back (via Route 100) along Route 125 over Middlebury Gap, you'll experience **spectacular back road driving** on your way to Middlebury. This path is especially recommended in autumn when every inch of the area is ablaze with color.

Otter Creek rushes through the center of **Middlebury**, a historic town otherwise defined by the Congregational Church steeple and hundreds of 18th and 19th century brick buildings – the mills and marble factories of yesteryear converted to a quaint shopping district full of boutiques, galleries and restaurants.

Middlebury is a real pleasure to stroll. The east side of town is focused on Main Street and its lovely downtown shopping strip. Smack in the center of town you can gaze down into the falls of **Otter Creek** from the Battell Bridge, then cross over to Cannon Park, which features its iron-clad namesake and a plaque commemorating local blacksmith and

SIGHTS

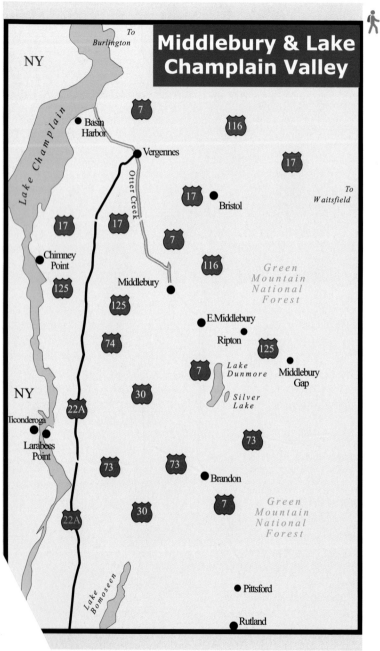

Middlebury & Lake Champlain Valley

To Burlington

NY

Lake Champlain

Basin Harbor

Vergennes

Otter Creek

Bristol

To Waitsfield

Chimney Point

Middlebury

Green Mountain National Forest

E.Middlebury

Ripton

Lake Dunmore

Middlebury Gap

Silver Lake

NY

Ticonderoga

Larabees Point

Brandon

Green Mountain National Forest

Lake Bomoseen

Pittsford

Rutland

plowing pioneer John Deere. Continuing on the western side of Otter Creek leads you to the campus of **Middlebury College**. The state's most highly-esteemed university is a mix of modern buildings and some historic marble ones nicknamed "Old Stone Row."

As befits a town with a top liberal arts school, Middlebury offers a wealth of cultural attractions. The oldest community history museum in the country, the venerable **Henry Sheldon Museum** displays marvelously odd artifacts from the collection of a 19th century pack rat. The college's **Museum of Art's** modern complex holds everything from modern painting to Asian antiquities. And the most artful setting of all may belong to the **Frog Hollow State Craft Center**, which showcases the work of local artisans in an old mill building overlooking Otter Creek Falls.

Info: *Henry Sheldon Museum*
1 Park St
Open Tues.-Sat. 10am-5pm and Sun. 1-5pm in summer
Admission $5
Tel. 802-388-2117
www.henrysheldonmuseum.org.
Middlebury College Museum of Art, Mahaney Center for the Arts
Open Tues.-Fri. 10am-5pm, Sat.-Sun. 12-5pm
Admission free. Tel. 802-443-5007
www.middlebury.edu/arts/museum
Frog Hollow Craft Center
1 Main St. Tel. 802-388-3177
www.froghollow.org

Middlebury's fondness for craft extends even to its signature brewery, **Otter Creek**, which makes small batches of its celebrated ales (and its organic sideline, Wolaver's) at its steel vat-framed headquarters just north of town. Its tasting room dispenses

SIGHTS

SIGHTS

samples of regional favorites like the Stovepipe Porter, and free tours are offered in the afternoon. *Info*: 793 Exchange St. Open Tues.-Sat. 10 am-6 pm. Tel. 802-388-0727. www.ottercreekbrewing.com.

Whether you overindulge at Otter Creek or just want to drink in the surroundings a little more, spending the night in Middlebury is worth considering. There are some **great inns** in the area – the elegant **Swift House** being one of the best (*see Sleeps & Eats section below*) – and enough activities outside of town to merit a second and even a third day.

Lake Champlain is just a half hour's drive north and west from Middlebury. Prime outdoor opportunities, especially in and around **Button Bay State Park**, are there for the taking, and just past the town of Vergennes is the **Lake Champlain Maritime Museum**. Here you can board a replica gunboat, take a virtual tour of a 19th century schooner and peruse pier-side exhibits chronicling the early of the Burlington water-

Info: Button Bay State Park
Off Route 22A, Ferrisburgh
Open mid May-Oct.
Lake Champlain Maritime Museum
4472 Basin Harbor Rd., Vergennes
Open daily 10am-5pm late May-mid Oct
Admission $10
Tel. 802-475-2022
www.lcmm.org

A visit to the Maritime Museum dovetails well with an excursion further north to the **Rokeby Museum** in Ferrisburgh. A lovely 20-minute trip from Middlebury via Route 7, this hilltop homestead is a National Historic Landmark that offers considerable insights into 19th century rural

life. Once home to an abolitionist family, the 90-acre farm was a stop on the Underground Railroad, and the premises feature exhibits on Civil War era history alongside hiking trails and agricultural attractions such as a creamery and smokehouse.

Info: *4334 Route 7, Ferrisburgh*
Open Thurs.-Sun. mid May-mid Oct
Admission $6
Tel. 802-877-3406
www.rokeby.org

Another lakeside excursion, due west of Middlebury via Route 125, involves **Chimney Point**. Once a strategic Lake Champlain crossing point, it's now best known for its extreme lake vistas and the Chimney Point State Historic Site. Its exhibits are set in an 18th century tavern and emphasize the area's Native American and French Canadian heritage. Chimney Point makes a great midpoint in a **scenic driving loop** from Middlebury. Take Route 125 out to the point and return via Route 17 for a beautiful glimpse into the surrounding countryside.

Info Chimney Point State

Historic Site
7305 Route 125, Addison
Open Wed.-Sun. 9:30am-5pm late May-mid Oct
Admission $3
Tel. 802-759-2412

Back closer to town, the **Morgan Horse Farm** is on a winding road just three miles from Middlebury in Weybridge. The 215-acre National Historic Site is maintained by the University of Vermont and features guided stable tours and presentations on America's first breed of horse. There are number of family farms in the area that are worth exploring too. **Apple Ridge Farms** in Shoreham is just 12 miles outside town and is one of Vermont's most beautiful rural properties. Clydesdales and bison roam its pastures, and its acres of orchards are ideal for fruit picking or a horse drawn tour.

Info: Morgan Horse Farm
74 Battell Dr., Weybridge
Open daily 9am-4pm May-Oct
Tel. 802-388-2011
www.uvm.edu/morgan
Apple Ridge Farms
1623 Buttolph Rd., Shoreham
Tel. 802-382-9338
www.appleridgefarms.com

SIGHTS

The area's most famous piece of land once belonged to the poet **Robert Frost**, who summered for nearly a quarter century in nearby **Ripton**. His farmhouse and cabin still remain, and the mile long Frost Interpretive Trail is one of the most leisurely – and certainly the most literary – little hikes in Vermont. Annotated with wooden posts bearing snippets of his work, the trail leads over a quaint wooden bridge and through stands of birch, blueberry bushes and other hallmarks of Frost imagery. Access to the trail is from Route 125 seven miles south of junction with 116. Don't let it be your road not taken.

The Frost homestead is just one of the attractions in the enormous **Green Mountain National Forest**, which is directly east of Middlebury and Route 7 and stretches north from Killington all the way up to Waitsfield. A true four season destination, the forest bursts with birdsong in spring and ignites with color in autumn. Prime spots for hiking re include the Mt. salamoo and Burnt Hill . By car over the course ple days, you can skirt e forest from Route 7

to Route 17, continuing over the top of the forest, turning south just past Waitsfield on Route 100 and returning to Killington through Warren, Hancock and Rochester.

At the crest of the forest's northeast reach is the **Mad River Valley** (see map in next chapter). One of the most pastoral stretches of the state, its hillside farms are framed by flowing streams, mountain ridges and the villages of **Waitsfield** and **Warren**. To see the heart of the valley, follow Route 100 between these two towns and then circle around via the East Warren Road. This is a ridiculously beautiful ride that you can do in little more than an hour, though you'll ideally take additional time to explore the back roads to your heart's content.

Set along the Mad River, Warren and Waitsfield have

both retained their original 19th century character. The southernmost of the two, Warren is characterized by its historic village center and the **Warren Covered Bridge** while Waitsfield is a bustling hamlet with small shops, one straight-up steeple spire and rustically **welcoming accommodations** at the Yellow Farmhouse and the Inn at Round Barn Farm (*see below for details*).

As authentic as these towns are, the primary reason to come to the valley is still the outdoors. Versatile trails such as the **Mad River Greenway** – which starts north of Waitsfield and runs along the Mad River – provide scenic views of the valley and the Green Mountains, and a pair of storied ski destinations – **Mad River Glen** and **Sugarbush** – lure snow hounds of all skill levels. Mad River Glen is one of the least developed mountain experiences available to serious skiers (see the alternate weekend plan for details), while Sugarbush strikes

a fine balance between the mountain megaplexes of the south and the more remote options to the north.

Located to the west side of the valley outside Warren, Sugarbush celebrated its 50th anniversary in 2008, and it's made numerous upgrades in the years leading up to that milestone. Its 111 trails snake along Lincoln Peak and Mount Ellen, two separate peaks that are linked by a high-speed quad. Golf, tennis and other outdoor activities are available year-round as well.

Info: 1840 Sugarbush Access Rd., Warren
Tel. 800-537-8427
www.sugarbush.com

BEST SLEEPS & EATS

KILLINGTON-RUTLAND
Highridge Condominiums $$$

Mountain views and modern amenities make Highridge the best high-end choice in Killington. The multi-room condos (some with loft) offer luxuries such as stone fireplaces, saunas and whirlpool tubs alongside extended stay practicalities such as a full kitchen and washer/dryer. The hillside location feels secluded relative to the rest of the resort yet is connected by both a ski-home trail and free shuttle service that links you to the slopes and the nightlife of Killington Road. Between the mountain vistas and the on-site outdoor options (clay tennis courts, a 20-person hot tub), however, you may not want to go anywhere else. *Info: www.killington.com. Tel. 802-442-6200. 180 High Ridge Rd. 128 rooms.*

Killington Grand Resort Hotel $$$

Among the top ski hotels in the country, the Killington Grand recently received a $2.5 million makeover and has a prime  location right on the mountain and a stone's throw from the golf course. Accommodations range from studio rooms to penthouses, and the list of amenities runs longer than lift lines on a holiday. Spa and health club services are world-class, and the 75-foot outdoor heated pool, with two hot bs and views of Killington Peak, epitomizes mountainside ury at its finest. *Info: www.killington.com. Tel. 802-442-〇. 228 E. Mountain Rd. 198 rooms.*

Ridge Inn $$-$$$

d to this classic A-frame lodge leads through a covered

carriageway and stands of silver and white birch. The A-frames contain a dining room and a slate and cedar great room with 20-foot ceilings, a fireplace and a small bar while guest rooms are spread throughout the central building. Clean and comfortable, they range from the Colonial room with maple armoire and spindle bed to the French provincial room with fireplace and whirlpool for two. *Info: www.birchridge.com. 37 Butler Rd. Tel. 802-422-4293. 10 rooms.*

Inn of the Six Mountains $$-$$$

Just one mile from Killington Resort, this AAA three diamond property fancies itself a resort too, albeit on a smaller, much less luxurious scale. The location is great, and public areas, from the fireplaced lobby to Cedars Restaurant, are welcoming. Deluxe rooms have standard amenities and a hint of home while deck and balcony rooms offer outdoor access and superior décor. *Info: www.sixmountains.com. Tel. 802-422-4302. 2617 Killington Rd. 103 rooms.*

The Inn at Rutland $$-$$$

A ten-minute walk to town, this inn occupies a restored 1889 Victorian mansion on a main road that's also just a short ride from Killington. A good compromise between the resort and a motel, a stay here comes with a full breakfast, character-filled common areas and a wrap-around porch that looks out onto the Green Mountains. The dining room features antiques and a plaster relief ceiling, and the

Bennington guest room has a private balcony. *Info: www.innatrutland.com. Tel. 800-808-0575. 70 N. Main St., Rutland. 8 rooms.*

Holiday Inn Rutland $$

Conveniently located on Route 7 near its junction with Route 4, this locally owned outpost of the national chain is among its best.

The recently renovated lobby incorporates Vermont stone and other local elements, and guest rooms and suites have all been spruced up within the last few years and offer a choice of king or two double beds. *Info: www.hivermont.com. Tel. 802-775-1911. 476 Route 7 South, Rutland. 151 rooms.*

Mountain Inn $$

The Mountain Inn is popular both for its accessible location and energetic après-ski scene. Guest rooms are nothing special, though the deluxe variety with fireplace and balcony adds mountain views and a modicum of warmth. Gathering spots include a lounge with stone fireplace, a pub and outdoor heated pool. *Info: www.mtninn.com. Tel. 802-422-3595. 1 Killington Rd. 51 rooms.*

Hemingway's $$$

Hemingway's moveable feasts are served in three different yet equally charming areas: a chandeliered main dining room; stone walled wine cellar; and fireplaced back room. The cuisine has made *Food and Wine's* Top 25 and ranges from multi-course and wine tasting menus (including a four-course vegetarian menu) to straight-up specialties such as Vermont pheasant with house-made gnocchi. *Info: 4988 Route 4. Tel. 802-422-3886. Dinner Tues.-Sun. www.hemingwaysrestaurant.com.*

Ovations $$$

The Killington Grand's dining room and adjacent Rendezvous lounge gets a standing ovation as the mountain's most convenient fine dining option. The menu features a dozen entrees (steaks, Kobe burger, fisherman's stew), and more casual, pub-style fare is served in the lounge. *Info: 228 E. Mountain Rd. Tel. '02-422-6111. Breakfast and dinner daily. www.killington.com.*

Garlic $$

tzatziki to tempura, this multi-ethnic, tapas-style restaurant has of everything. The aroma of its namesake bulb is detectable the entrance, and its flavor is apparent in shellfish dishes and e potato soup. *Info: 1724 Killington Rd. Tel. 802-422-5055. iily. www.thegarlicinkillington.com.*

Peppino's Ristorante $$

From classic pastas to parmigianas, Peppino's offes an appealing Italian bistro menu that also includes specials such as linguine topped with mussels and fried calamari. The wine list and good-humored wait staff are also pluses. *Info: Killington Access Rd. Tel. 802-422-3293. Dinner daily. www.peppinoskillington.com.*

Table 24 $$

Rough wood textures and smooth terra cotta walls suit this relatively new, chef-owned eatery in Rutland. Reasonable yet gourmet, it specializes in comfort food (pot roast, five cheese macaroni) and meats cooked on the wood-fired rotisserie. *Info: 24 Wales St., Rutland. Tel. 802-775-2424. Lunch and dinner Mon.-Sat. www.table24.net.*

Back Home Again Café $

Run by members of a religious group called the Twelve Tribes, this health-con-scious café serves delicious light fare out of a beautifully rustic wooden building in Rutland. Vines and plants snake up the interior walls, and a chalk-  board announces a range of fresh juices, smoothies and maté drinks. Wednesday nights bring pizza specials and live music. *Info: 23 Center St., Rutland. Tel. 802-775-9800. Lunch and dinner Mon.-Thurs., lunch Fri., Sun. www.backhomeagaincafe.com.*

Outback Pizza $

Alligators and snakes adorn the menu of this dangerously delicious pizza joint. Pizza's pretty much the only thing on the menu, but with a dozen custom pies and a 2-for-1 happy hour special, why would you order anything else? *Info: 2841 Killington Rd. Tel. 802-422-9885. Lunch and dinner daily. www.killingtonsbest.com.*

SLEEPS & EATS

SLEEPS & EATS

MIDDLEBURY
Inn on the Green $$-$$$

Set on the town green just a five minute stroll from Middlebury College, this Federal style inn is on the National Register of Historic Places. The guest rooms are named for surrounding towns and feature quaint luxuries such as cannonball beds and handmade quilts. Carriage house rooms are colorful with a hint of the contemporary, and a pair of suites are available for larger groups. All rooms come with private bath and the possibility of a complimentary continental breakfast in bed. *Info: www.innonthegreen.com. Tel. 802-388-7512. 71 S. Pleasant St. 11 rooms.*

Swift House Inn $$-$$$

Once the governor's mansion, today's Swift House is a lovely three building inn with a library, gardens and a restaurant that

serves candlelit dinners. Rooms in the nook-filled main house are the most quaint while the more modern carriage house offers additional luxuries like king beds, Jacuzzi tubs and private patios. Half a mile down the road from the main inn, the Gate House is the most affordable option here. Location and road noise reduce its rates but not the charm of its ornate woodwork, turreted guest rooms and Victorian wraparound porch. *Info: www.swifthouseinn.com. Tel. 802-388-9925. 25 Stewart Ln. 20 rooms.*

ipman Inn $$

in the mountains above Middlebury, this white house with 'ers is a classically welcoming farmhouse inn. Timelessly - Robert Frost's old retreat is two miles down the road, and a red clapboard country store across the street – the area ≥nse of timelessness about it that's reinforced by the innkeepers, who have owned the property for the past 25 years. The main lounge area has an original fireplace and private bar, and the library and guest rooms (which range from a small single room to a suite) are cozy and comfortably furnished with antiques. *Info: www.chipmaninn.com. Tel. 802-388-2390. Route 125, Ripton. 8 rooms.*

Black Sheep Bistro $$-$$$
About 15 minutes northwest of Middlebury, this gem of a French bistro is well worth the trip up Route 7. Decorated with French prints and with a lovely patio in summer, it provides superior "gourmet casual" ambiance, food and service. Round number pricing (all entrees $19 as of this printing) and an outstanding yet affordable wine list makes the tab as easy to digest as the creative appetizers and entrees, which range from lamb and hanger steak specialties to snacky indulgences like French fries with a trio of custom condiments. *Info: 253 Main St., Vergennes. Tel. 802-877-9991. Dinner daily.*

Fire & Ice $$-$$$
More hot than cold, Fire & Ice's menu is so loaded with steak and prime rib options that it has special sections on cuts and cooking methods. The early bird menu is a great deal, as is the huge salad bar, which is a dinner unto itself. *Info: 26 Seymour St. Tel. 802-388-7166. Lunch Fri.-Sun., dinner daily. www.fireandicerestaurant.com.*

Tully & Marie's $$
Overlooking Otter Creek, this multi-ethnic eatery serves Asian, Mexican and Italian entrees alongside great sandwiches and seafood specials. Meat and vegetarian options are abundant, and tofu can be substituted into signature dishes such as ginger cashew chicken. *Info: 7 Bakery Ln. Tel. 802-388-4182. Lunch and dinner daily. www.tullyandmaries.com.*

Mister Up's $-$$
Another casual waterfront spot, Mister Up's is popular for its screened-in porch, nightly specials and a huge menu of appetizers and heartier fare. A lengthy drink list and late-serving kitchen (till midnight on weekends) endear it to night owls in particular.

Info: 25 Bakery Ln. Tel. 802-3886724. Lunch and dinner daily. www.misterupsvt.com.

Dinky Donuts $

Old-fashioned, handmade donuts made with local products and sold out of a small red schoolhouse – need I say more? Coffee, breads, pastries and soups are also available, and if your timing's off, the company does mail order too. *Info: 1663 Route 7 South. Tel. 802-839-5099. Open Wed.-Sun. 7 am-2 pm. www.eatdinkydonuts.com.*

Otter Creek Bakery $

A great lunch stop on the edge of campus, this European-style

bakery/deli serves a host of sandwiches on six different house-baked breads. Soups, patés, salads and baked goods are all delicious and reasonably priced. *Info: 14 College St. Tel. 802-388-3371. Open daily. www.ottercreekbakery.com.*

MAD RIVER VALLEY

Clay Brook at Sugarbush $$$

Part of the Lincoln Peak Village complex (along with the Gatehouse Base Lodge and Timbers Restaurant) that opened at Sugarbush in 2006, this all-suites hotel provides four-star luxury accommodations in the shadow of the mountain. The one to five-bedroom suites contain four-poster beds, hardwood furniture and fireplaces as well as kitchens with granite counters and stainless steel ppliances. Additional amenities include a racquet club, a yearund outdoor heated pool and hot tub, and boot warming services winter. *Info: www.sugarbush.com. Tel. 800-537-8427. 102 st Dr., Warren. 110 rooms.*

Round Barn Farm $$$

d River Valley's classiest country inn is set on 245 acres s, fields, gardens and trails. Listed as a National Historic namesake round barn is used mostly for special events, but the 19th century farmhouse and adjacent restored horse barn feels every bit as timeless. The fireplaced living room, game room and outdoor patio invite lounging, and guest rooms ably blend country comfort (original wood beams, gas fireplaces) and modern luxury (steam showers, Tempurpedic beds). Each room is unique, from the window walled Sterling Room to the Richardson Room with skylight and vaulted

beam ceiling. *Info: www.theroundbarnfarm.com. Tel. 802-496-2276. 1661 E. Warren Rd., Waitsfield. 12 rooms.*

West Hill House $$-$$$

High-character common areas distinguish this flag-fronted clapboard inn set on a forest-surrounded country road just one mile from Sugarbush and seven from Mad River Glen. The three fireplaced lounge areas include a cozy brick and hardwood library that's ideal for reading or shooting pool. With exposed beams, pine floors and country quilts, guest rooms exude a similar charm. Try the Highland Room, which nods to the innkeeper's Scottish heritage with rustic barn board walls and a set of mounted bagpipes. *Info: www.westhillbb.com. Tel. 802-496-7162. 1496 West Hill Rd., Warren. 8 rooms.*

Sugarbush Village $$-$$$

Offering one to four-bedroom condo stays at the base of mountain, this rental company specializes in ski-on, ski-off lodging and group accommodations. An on-site reception center offers personal service and a gathering space with wi-fi. *Info: www.sugarbushvillage.com. 72 Mountainside Dr., Warren. Tel. 800-451-4326. 12 rooms.*

SLEEPS & EATS

SLEEPS & EATS

Yellow Farmhouse $$

Set on 10 acres just off of Route 100, this sunny bed and breakfast

offers eight comfortable guest rooms with views of the surrounding gardens, fields and the mountains. Sleep soundly in the second floor Stephanie room's cherry four-poster bed or opt for the blue and white Nicole room with Jacuzzi tub. Some rooms have Vermont Castings stoves, and all come with a full three-course breakfast. *Info: www.yellowfarmhouseinn.com. Tel. 802-496-4263. 550 Old County Rd., Waitsfield. 8 rooms.*

Sugar Lodge at Sugarbush $$

Less than half a mile from Sugarbush, this mountain lodge is a convenient and affordable option for families and travelers who plan to spend more time in the mountains than at the hotel. Standard rooms are small but a great value, and stepping up to a select room nets you exposed beams and additional space. Guests often gather around the Great Room's fireplace and in the outdoor pool and hot tub. *Info: www.sugarlodge.com. Tel. 802-583-3300. 2197 Sugarbush Access Rd., Warren. 23 rooms.*

Hyde Away $-$$

Located between Warren and Waitsfield, this 1824 farmstead turned lodge offers private rooms with bath as well as shared, bunk-style accommodations. Common areas include a casual tavern and a living room with couches and a television. *Info: www.hydeawayinn.com. Tel. 802-496-2322. 1428 Mill Brook Rd., Waitsfield. 10 rooms.*

Chez Henri $$$

Henri himself still helms this French restaurant that's been a Valley favorite since 1964. Known for its impeccable service and old-fashioned European feel, the intimate, candlelit dining room serves Parisian classics such as beef au poivre, French onion soup and fondue, and there's a less formal bistro menu as well. Reservations are recommended, as is requesting a table by the fire. *Info: Sugarbush Village, Warren. Tel. 802-583-2600. Lunch and dinner daily in season.*

Timbers Restaurant $$$

Part of Sugarbush's Lincoln Peak Village complex, this high-end restaurant is attached to the Clay Brook all-suites hotel and across from the Gate House base lodge. The round barn setting is as rustically elegant as the menu, which features seafood, four kinds of steak and a "ski fuel" lunch menu. *Info: Lincoln Peak Village, Warren. Tel. 802-583-6800. Breakfast, lunch and dinner daily. www.sugarbush.com.*

Common Man $$-$$$

Dine beneath the rafters in this 19th century barn set between Lincoln Peak and Mount Ellen. Romantic country ambiance (chandeliers, roaring open fire) enhances the locally informed New England cuisine. Try the grilled quail or the beggar's purse of phyllo-wrapped escargot and blue cheese. Deluxe entrees and a smaller bistro menu are available, and both are a good value for such a superlative dining experience. *Info: 3209 German Flats Rd., Warren. Tel. 802-583-2800. Dinner Tues.-Sat. www.commonmanrestaurant.com.*

American Flatbread $$

Vermont's best pizza bakers turn their Waitsfield dough-house into a restaurant on weekends. Dine on their well-topped flatbread pies as the bakers knead and the oven fire crackles around you. *Info: 46 Lareau Rd., Waitsfield. Tel. 802-496-8856. Dinner Fri.-Sat. www.americanflatbread.com.*

Big Picture Theater and Café $$

It's easy to make an event of a meal at the Big Picture, where there are as many entertainment as dining options. A jazz brunch, a disco night, an outdoor beer garden and a full-on movie theater make the menu of salads, steaks, tapas and Dagwood-style sandwiches that much more invigorating. Breakfast is served till 3 pm. *Info: 48*

Carroll Rd., Waitsfield. Tel. 802-496-8994. Breakfast, lunch and dinner Wed.-Sun. www.bigpicturetheater.info.

Green Cup Café $-$$$

The Valley's best little café recently branched out into dinner. Pastries, quiche and sandwich specials are still offered by day, and on Saturday through Monday nights, the space transforms into a gourmet dining experience. The menu breaks down the flavors, ingredients and technique that go into each of the dishes, which include grass-fed ribeye, Spanish mackerel and a must-order coconut cake. *Info: 40 Bridge St., Waitsfield. Tel. 802-496-4963. Breakfast and lunch Fri.-Tues., dinner Sat.-Mon. www.greencupvermont.com.*

Michael's Good to Go $

This high-character hole-in-the-wall only does take out, and its wraps, salads and soups are perfect for a quick meal or quality picnic. For something more substantial, try the locally produced farm dinner and key lime pie – it beats many sit down restaurants' best. *Info: 2 Village Sq., Waitsfield. Tel. 802-496-3832. Lunch Tues.-Fri., dinner Thurs.-Sat.*

BEST SHOPPING

Killington
Killington Outfitters (*Route 4*) stocks a huge selection of mountain gear and other outdoor accessories, and smaller Killington Sports outposts are located in all the base lodges to serve more basic and rental needs. Off-resort, you'll also find a number of outdoor outfitters and other businesses along Killington Road.

Rutland is the nearest commercial center to Killington. Though largely populated by chains and box stores, it does offer some high-character shopping centered on Center Street and Merchants Row. For a complete list of shops in the area visit *www.rutlandvermont.com.*

Farm stands and **general stores** populate the surrounding countryside

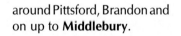

around Pittsford, Brandon and on up to **Middlebury**.

The latter's quaint shopping district is the most cosmopolitan in the area. Peruse the boutiques and galleries lining **Main Street** and the

specialty stores in the **Marble Works** (*on Maple St.*), and don't miss the **Frog Hollow State Crafts Center** (*1 Mill St.*), which displays fantastic work by local artists and artisans in a spectacular falls-side setting. As befitting a college town, Middlebury also has more than its share of great bookstores. **The Vermont Book Shop** (*38 Main St.*) and **Monroe Street Books** (*70 Monroe St.*) are both beloved by bibliophiles. For

more information, visit *www.midvermont.com.*

Mad River Valley
The villages of **Waitsfield** and **Warren** are the centers of the Valley's consumer activity. **Clearwater Sports** (*4147 Main St.*) in Waitsfield is a good outdoor outfitter, and you can also shop for art and crafts at the nearby **Artisans' Gallery** (*Bridge St.*) or the **Collection** in the Mad River Green shopping center (*Route 100*). Warren also has its share of craft and antique dealers. Perhaps no artisan's shop in the Valley is more unusual than **Mad River Antler**, a by-appointment-only (*Tel. 802-496-9290, www.madriverantler.com*) boutique shop that creates furniture, light fixtures and other home accessories from antler sheds. For more information, visit *www.madrivervalley.com.*

NIGHTLIFE & ENTERTAINMENT

BEST NIGHTLIFE & ENTERTAINMENT

Killington

Killington has hands-down the biggest nightlife scene of any Vermont resort. In fact, the promise of popular après-ski spots such as **Mahogany Ridge** (*at the Killington Base Lodge*) and the **Bear Mountain Lounge** (*at Bear Mountain Base Lodge*) may have you hurtling down the slopes that much faster. Out on Killington Road, the party goes all night at nightclubs like the **Wobbly Barn** (*2229 Killington Rd., Tel. 802-422-6171*) and the Pickle Barrel (*1741 Killington Rd., Tel. 802-422-3035*). Three levels of bars, live music and an active dance floor make the latter particularly popular.

Killington Road also features a few lower-key nightspots as well, including **Casey's Caboose** (*Tel. 802-422-3795*) and the **Grist Mill** (*Tel. 802-422-3970*).

Middlebury

The classy **Two Brothers Tavern** (*86 Main St., Tel. 802-388-0002*) makes a perfect night out. It serves outstanding pub fare alongside a wide range of microbrews and selections from its notorious "shotski". **Otter Creek Brewing**, one of Vermont's finest craft brewers, also has its headquarters (*793 Exchange St., Tel. 800-473-0727*) just north of the town center. You can sample a range of ales and porters as well as its organic side line, Wolaver's, at the tasting room Tuesday through Saturday, but you'll have to do it before 6 pm.

Middlebury's performing arts scene is excellent. The **Town Hall Theater** (*54 Main St., Tel. 802-388-1436*) hosts music, dance and opera events year-round, and there's always something going on at Middlebury College venues

RIDE SERVICES FROM KILLINGTON

Some Killington night spots offer complimentary shuttle service to and from their clubs to make sure you get home safely at the end of the night. The **Pickle Barrel's Barrel Rider** (*Tel. 802-422-7433*) and **Wobbly Barn's Wobbly Wagon** (*Tel. 800-847-2276*) are two of the most popular.

such as the **Wright Theater** and the **Mahaney Center for the Arts**. Check listings at *www.middlebury.edu/arts* for more information.

Rutland

Rutland's best performing arts venue is the **Paramount Theater** (*30 Center St., Tel. 802-775-0570*), a beautifully restored downtown hall that once hosted Harry Houdini and Groucho Marx and features a regular schedule of musical and theatrical events. If your timing is right, seasonal activities in Rutland are worth considering too, from the **Vermont State Fair** in September to **Wilson Castle's "After Dark" series** of theatrical murder mystery dinners. Happening from May through October, they feature a cocktail hour, formal dinner and intimate acquaintance with the one-of-a-kind castle (*W. Proctor Rd., Tel. 802-773-3284*).

Mad River Valley

Sugarbush's après-ski scene (*photo at right*) starts at the base lodge's **Castlerock Pub** – which offers live music and banks of high-definition televisions – and extends to local off-mountain haunts such as the **Hyde Away** (*1428 Millbrook Rd., Tel. 802-496-2322*). **General Stark's Pub** (*Mad River Glen base area*) is that resort's prime après-ski spot.

With a hand-wrought mahogany bar and nightly drink specials, the **Purple Moon Pub** in Warren (*Route 100, Tel. 802-496-3422*) is a popular village gathering place, as is the **Big Picture Theater Café** in Waitsfield (*48 Carroll St., Tel. 802-496-8994*). It screens first-run movies nightly and hosts karaoke and disco nights on weekends. Waitsfield's **Valley Players troupe** heads the Valley's small performing arts scene, with the "Cabin Fever Follies" variety show and the **Mad River Unplugged** folk and blues series among its standout events (*4254 Main St., Tel. 802-583-1674*).

BEST SPORTS & RECREATION

Killington

Two hundred slopes, 31 lifts, 87 miles of terrain, six freestyle parks – no wonder **Killington Resort** is known as the "Beast of the East." The largest ski resort in eastern North America has trails for every skill level, from the Snowshed beginner area to the double black diamond **Big Dipper Glade**. The superpipe on **Bear Mountain** and the brand-new **Stash terrain park** are just two of the highlights awaiting snowboarders. For a less crowded alternative , try the trails on adjacent **Pico Peak**. Should you need guidance at any point, Snowshed ski ambassadors are stationed all over the resort and lead free daily tours of the slopes.

Golfers will also find a lot to love in Killington. The Geoffrey Cornish-designed **Killington Golf Course** offers mountain-surrounded fairways, a 14-station driving range and a 12,000-square foot putting green, while *Golf Digest* recently cited the off-resort **Green Mountain National Golf Course** (*Barrows Town Rd., Tel. 888-483-4683*) as the state's best public course.

KILLINGTON SHUTTLE

Finished your runs at a base different than the one you started at? No problem – the **Killington Bus** connects all seven base lodge parking lots and also makes frequent trips down Killington Road and to the various resort properties. *Info*: www.thebus.com/routes/killington.htm.

In summer, another set of outdoor attractions await. Spread across five mountain areas, the **Kona "Groove Approved" Mountain Bike Park** offers over

45 miles of terrain, a 1,700-foot vertical drop and full rental fleet of downhill and trail bikes. Thrills abound at the **Pico Mountain Adventure Center**, which offers a climbing wall, bungee jumping and alpine slides. For a more relaxed taste of the outdoors, take a leisurely hike up **Deer Leap Mountain** or a guided horseback ride with **Pico Mountain Stables**. For information on outdoor activities in and around Killington, visit *www.killington.com*.

Away from the resort, the gigantic **Green Mountain National Forest** extends from Killington's back yard all the way past Middlebury and north to Waitsfield. The **Long Trail** runs through the forest, as do other fine trails such as **Burnt Hill** and **Mount Moosalamoo**. The **Robert Frost Interpretive Trail** in Ripton is the area's most pleasant – and educational – hiking experience. All told, you can spend countless days exploring the forest, and a well-maintained network of campgrounds allows you stay past nightfall.

Mad River Valley

Encompassing **Lincoln Peak** and **Mount Ellen**, **Sugarbush** is the Valley's largest ski resort (*off Route 100, Warren, www.sugarbush.com*). A total of 16 lifts connect a network of 111 trails with appeal to all skill levels. The 2,600-foot vertical drop, trio of terrain parks and backwoods ski opportunities all bring a sense of mountain adventure, and golf, tennis and hiking on the Long Trail give the resort appeal in all seasons.

THE SINGLE CHAIR LIFT!

Mad River Glen's historic single chair lift began carrying skiers up General Stark Mountain in 1948. It was cutting-edge technology then, but today it's one of only two solo lifts in the country (and the only one in its original location). A $1.5 million restoration concluded in 2008, ensuring that skiers will be riding the Mad River icon for many years to come.

Cooperatively-owned **Mad River Glen** (*off Route 17, www.madriverglen.com*) provides Vermont's most authentic mountain experience. There's no snowboarding and little to no snowmaking here – just straight-up ski slopes with an emphasis on the expert. Wooded trails follow General Stark Mountain's natural counters and are served by five lifts, including the resort's iconic single chair.

Elsewhere in the Valley, you can take the Long Trail up **Burnt Rock Mountain** (*trail starts at the end of Big Basin Road*) for a memorably challenging hike, or follow the **Mad River Greenway trail** along the river from its head north of Waitsfield. It offers spectacular, mid-grade hiking, biking and even a swimming hole. If you need some guidance, **Clearwater Sports** in Waitsfield (*4147 Main St., Tel. 802-496-2708*) leads river tours in summer and snowshoe treks in winter and also rents kayaks and other equipment. For an entirely different sort of tour, take a trail ride or overnight trek through the Valley with a **Vermont Icelandic Horse Farm** guide (*N. Fayston Rd. off Route 100, Tel. 802-496-7141*) or a dog sledding ride with the mushers at **Atii Sled Dogs** (*www.atiisleddogs.com*).

7. STOWE, WATERBURY & MONTPELIER

HIGHLIGHTS

▲ Stowe/Mount Mansfield

▲ Waterbury/Ben & Jerry's

▲ Montpelier

▲ Barre

▲ Skiing, Hiking

INTRO

Northwest Vermont's signature village, **Stowe** also offers some of Vermont's most dramatic and accessible outdoor recreation. Nestled in a valley surrounded by the Green Mountains and

COORDINATES

Stowe sits on **Rt. 100** about ten miles from the **Waterbury** exit (exit 10) off I-89. At Stowe, **Rt. 108** veers northwest to **Mt. Mansfield** and **Smuggler's Notch. Montpelier** is further south at the junction of I-89 and Rt. 2.

Vermont's highest peak, **Mount Mansfield**, it's half small town, half ski mecca, with as many rustic, unassuming inns as topnotch resorts. The surrounding area is just as full of attractions and natural beauty, with highlights ranging from the **Ben & Jerry's** ice cream factory in **Waterbury** to the historic state capital, **Montpelier**.

SIGHTS

STOWE SIGHTS IN A DAY

Founded in 1794, the once-sleepy hamlet of **Stowe** is today a polished, consumer-friendly tourist destination that requires no sacrifice of scenery in exchange for its multitude of shops and first class amenities.

Spend the first part of your day getting to know them with a morning stroll through **Stowe Village**. Inns and restaurants cluster along Main Street and Mountain Road, along with a pleasingly craft-centric set of **shops and galleries** that includes the artisan-supplied Stowe Craft Gallery and Design Center and the contemporary West

Branch Gallery and Sculpture Park. The white-steepled Stowe Community Church is the village's most picturesque architectural landmark.

Info: Stowe Craft Gallery and Design Center
55 Mountain Rd
Tel. 877-456-8388
www.stowecraft.com
West Branch Gallery and Sculpture Park
17 Towne Farm Ln
Tel. 800-253-8953
www.westbranchgallery.com
Stowe Community Church
137 S. Main St

Beginning just behind the church is the **Stowe Recre-**

SIGHTS

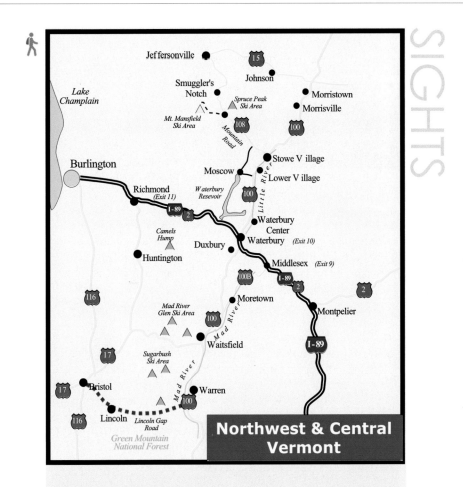

Northwest & Central Vermont

ation Path, a 5.5-mile all-purpose trail extending from the village to the covered bridge on Mountain Road. Perfect for leisurely walking, biking or cross country skiing, this scenic paved path winds along the West Branch River, past farmland, swimming holes and alluring glimpses of **Mt. Mansfield**. The path's flat terrain and proximity to town – it essentially runs parallel to Route 108 – make it ideal for all fitness levels and for strolls short and long.

By early afternoon the views of Mt. Mansfield from town and the path will have demanded a closer view. Rising to an elevation of nearly 4,400

SIGHTS

feet, Mansfield's majestic both in its snow-capped face and for the sweeping views it affords of the surrounding area, with Lake Champlain to the west and New Hampshire's Mt. Washington to the east.

Hiking Mansfield is a thrill – and one highly recommended in the one-week plan – but with limited time, you'll be forgiven for taking the easy way up. The best way to drink in these dramatic views is via the **Gondola Skyride** to the summit. The toll road to the top is an efficient option when time is of more essence than the mountain air.

Info: Gondola Skyrides
Admission $14-22 round trip
Open 10 am-5 pm mid June-mid Oct.
Toll road
Admission $23 per car
Open 9 am-4 pm late May-late Oct

Tel. 802-253-3500
www.stowe.com

Mansfield may be Vermont's #1 mountain, but the state's most visited tourist attraction is actually the **Ben & Jerry's** ice cream factory in Waterbury. Less than 10 miles south via Route 100, it packs 190,000 pints a day while attracting more than a quarter million visitors annually with free samples and its unique corporate blend of entrepreneurship and social responsibility.

Ben and Jerry's makes a perfect afternoon jaunt from Stowe and is a can't miss for anyone traveling with kids. The half-hour factory tours are short and sweet and give you the scoop on the ice cream manufacturing process, from the Spiral Hardener ice cream conveyor to the "Flavor Graveyard" out back. Tours start every 30 minutes and are at their best during the week when most of the company's ice cream is made. Sample it free in the FlavoRoom or indulge more fully in the scoop shop/ gift store.

Info: 1281 Route 100, one mile north of exit 10

Admission $3, children under 12 free
Open daily 10 am-6 pm Oct.-June; 9 am-9 pm mid-July to mid-Aug; 9 am-7 pm mid-Aug-late Oct. Last tour leaves one hour before close
Tel. 866-258-6877
www.benjerry.com

If you haven't spoiled your dinner, head into the town of Waterbury – just over a mile southwest of the factory via Route 100 – for a magical meal at the **Alchemist**. The best brewpub in a region full of them melds malt, hops and a hearty menu into one of Vermont's most casually memorable dining experiences. Housed in what was once the Waterbury Post Office, the Alchemist delivers seven house-made ales nightly. One need not love beer, however, to fall under the Alchemist's spell. Its imaginative pub fare and desserts – including a decadent maple porter pudding cake – delight teetotalers and beer geeks alike.

Info: 23 S. Main St
Tel. 802-244-4120
www.alchemistbeer.com

A WEEKEND AROUND STOWE & WATERBURY

For a relaxing and well-rounded weekend, spend Friday night and Saturday in Stowe, then devote Sunday to the numerous attractions in and around Waterbury.

Stowe offers some of the state's **premier hospitality**, so start the weekend off right by treating yourself to a top-notch meal. Whether you define that as high-end gourmet at **Solstice** or a hearty burger at the **Shed**, you're sure to find what you're seeking.

A full Saturday in Stowe affords ample time to browse the shops and galleries of **Stowe Village** – most of which are conveniently situated along **Mountain Road** and **Main Street** – and also to soak in the outdoors. Spend your morning shopping in the Village and consider treating yourself to an Old World brunch at the crêpe-style Dutch Pancake Café.

Info: 990 Mountain Rd
Tel. 802-253-8921

SIGHTS

You'll also want to carve out a bit of time to see the **Vermont Ski Museum**. Its informative exhibits span snowboarding to Nordic skiing and trace everything from mountain history to the evolution of ski equipment. Housed in the nearly 200-year old Town Hall at the intersection of Main Street and Mountain Road, the museum's also home to the Vermont Ski Hall of Fame.

Info: *1 S. Main St*
Open Wed.-Mon. 12-5 pm
Admission $3
Tel. 802-253-9911
www.vermontskimuseum.com

Come afternoon, trade the village sidewalks for a mountain trail. The Stowe area offers any number of compelling, partial-day hikes, and undertaking one is key to experiencing the town's refined yet rugged personality.

Casual hikers will find the **Stowe Recreation Path** sufficient to their outdoor needs. As described in the one-day plan, a stroll here dovetails perfectly with shopping and an all-around exploration of Stowe Village while exposing you to the town's waterway, covered bridge and other natural beauty. More serious hikers may prefer the **Sterling Pond** and **Stowe Pinnacle** trails described later in this chapter.

Whichever trek you settle on, you'll want to leave yourself enough time to hike (or take the gondola) to the top of the area's prime peak, Mount Mansfield. If you're traveling with kids, reward them for all that shopping and walking with a ride on the **Alpine Slide**, a luge-like 2,300 foot run down nearby Spruce Peak.

Info: *Gondola Skyrides*
Admission $14-22 round trip
Open 10 am-5 pm mid June-mid Oct.
Tel. 802-253-3500
www.stowe.com

With **50 + restaurants** and an active post-slopes social scene, Stowe remains vibrant into the night whatever your tastes. You can go European gourmet at the **Trapp Family Lodge Dining Room** or enjoy Stowe's best pizza and live music at **Piecasso** (*see Best Sleeps & Eats below*). The town's most unique evening entertainment option is its **guided lantern tours**. Delivered from an early settler's perspective, the one-hour walking tours – complete with 18th century replica lanterns – illuminate the village, local history and the personalities that shaped it.

Info: Lantern tours depart from the Stowe Visitors' Center, 51 Main St., at 6 pm
Dates vary by season
Tickets $9
Tel. 802-244-1173
www.stowelanterntours.com

Come Sunday, start off with Stowe's best synthesis of nature and commerce: the **Stowe Farmers' Market.** Forty-odd vendors fill the field on Mountain Road from 10am to 3pm each Sunday from May through October, and the result is Stowe's most vibrant outdoor marketplace. Local artists, farmers and musicians contribute their wares and talents, and most are happy to share some conversation too. Come for refreshing, small-town atmosphere, a handcrafted souvenir or just the biggest, sweetest blueberries you've ever tasted.

Info: Tel. 802-472-8027
www.stowefarmersmarket.com

Once you've filled up on the market's fresh foods, hop in the car for a taste of the surrounding countryside. **Route 108,** the area's most dramatic stretch of road, winds through the impossibly green **Mount Mansfield State Forest** on its way through Smuggler's Notch (aka "The Notch") and over the mountain to Jeffersonville. Switchbacking around a series of striking stone outcroppings, Route 108 demands cautious driving in the best of weather and closes for the winter at the season's first snow.

NOTCH CLOSED IN WINTER The winding **Smugglers' Notch Pass** on **Route 108** between Stowe and Jeffersonville is closed for winter travel from mid-October through mid-May. Beware of GPS and online directions services that may route you through the pass during that period. For an **alternate route,** follow Route 100 north through Stowe to Morrisville to Route 15 west, which leads through the town of Johnson to Jeffersonville.

Eleven miles from Stowe up Route 108 is the Sterling Pond

SIGHTS

Trail, a pristine ramble that's one of the region's very best mid-range hikes. Part of the **Long Trail**, this straightforward, initially steep hike starts at the pinnacle of the Notch and leads through stands of pine to the pond's strikingly beautiful shore. This is about a two hour hike top to bottom. For more, tack on the worthwhile two-hour loop around the pond's wooded edge via the Elephant's Head Trail, then link back with the Sterling Pond Trail to return to the trailhead. At an elevation of over 3,000 feet, Sterling Pond affords ample views of the mountains while generating considerable beauty of its own.

Once you've found your niche in the Notch, head back through Stowe Village to Route 100 south and the corridor known as **"Enticement Alley."** The ten mile stretch between Stowe and the town of Waterbury contains a trove of tourist attractions, the cream of the crop of which is the **Ben & Jerry's** ice cream factory. While it only produces ice cream Monday through Friday, Ben & Jerry's cranks out free samples seven days a week and as such re-mains a mandatory stop for families and anyone with a sweet tooth.

Info: 1281 Route 100, one mile north of exit 10
Admission $3, children under 12 free
Open daily 10am-6pm Oct.-June; 9am-9pm July to mid-Aug.; 9am-7pm mid-Aug.-late Oct. Last tour leaves one hour before close
Tel. 866-258-6877
www.benjerry.com

No less touristy but no less delicious is the **Cold Hollow Cider Mill**. Just up the road from Ben & Jerry's, the mill-cum-market – one of New England's top cider producers – offers fresh-pressed apple cider along with a warehouse-sized supply of Vermont products, gifts and specialty food items. Acquaint yourself with the company's old-fashioned cider-making process, then help yourself to free samples.

SIGHTS

You can get even more local flavor along Route 100 with a quick stop at the **Cabot Cheese Annex** or **Green Mountain Coffee**. The latter's visitors' center/ café occupies part of Waterbury's historic downtown train station. Characterized by stately old houses and a village green, Waterbury itself is also well worth a wander. Take in its low-key sites, including the attractive shops along Stowe Street, then put the finishing touches on your day with a pint at **The Alchemist** brewpub or a gourmet dinner at the **Hen of the Wood** restaurant (see *Best Sleeps & Eats*). Both raise the bar daily with high-class comfort food and an array of house-brewed ales.

While many of Cold Hollow's delicacies, such as its signature cider donuts, are available year-round, a visit during apple season remains ideal. Cold Hollow's production slows in warmer months, and when visiting during late summer, my humble cider requests have been met with a brusque "no apples, no cider."

Info: *Route 100, Waterbury Center*
Open daily 8am-6pm, 8am-7pm in summer
Admission free
Tel. 802-244-8771
www.coldhollow.com

Info: *Cabot Cheese Annex*
2657 Route 100
Tel. 802-244-6334
www.cabotcheese.com
Green Mountain Coffee
333 Meadow St
Tel. 877-879-2326
www.greenmountaincoffee.com
The Alchemist
23 S. Main St
Tel. 802-244-4120
www.alchemistbeer.com

SIGHTS

A WEEK IN STOWE, WATERBURY, & MONTPELIER

Spend your first two days in Stowe Village and Waterbury as outlined above, then extend your stay with visits to nearby towns and points of interest. Stagger your activities so that a day of hiking or skiing in the mountains is followed by a relaxing day at the lodge or a day trip to the historic state capital, **Montpelier**.

Just 22 miles from Stowe via I-89 and Route 2, Montpelier makes an ideal day-long excursion from your base in Stowe. The country's smallest state capital, Montpelier may also be its most livable, as it's an exceedingly walkable, welcoming town full of history, shops and restaurants.

Unassuming **Main Street** is Montpelier's most attractive commercial thoroughfare, populated as it is with first-rate galleries, craft shops and a number of excellent bookstores. Lined with Greek Revival, Italian Renaissance and Federal style buildings, it's as architecturally diverse as it is historic. Highlights abound along **State Street** as well, from handsome Federal style brick buildings to the Gothic Episcopal church. With its granite façade and chess-piece tower, the latter resembles something straight out of nineteenth century Britain.

A bit further down State Street is Montpelier's standout edifice: the golden-domed **State House** (*see photo above*). Set on a hilltop with an expanse of green lawn rolled out along its slope, It's the rare capital building that's as well suited to picnicking as politicking. People watch along the lawn, then head up the steps to see its columned entrance and gilded dome up close. Free guided tours, departing on the half hour, lead through the house's halls and chambers.

Info: 115 State St
Tel. 802-828-2228
Open Mon.-Sat., July-mid Oct; Mon.-Fri., mid Oct-June
Admission free

If the State House has whetted your appetite for local heritage, you can go even further back into state lore at the **Vermont Historical Society**. Located in a replica of the Pavilion Hotel, an architecturally striking structure just two doors east of the State House, this informative museum contains 400+ years' worth of Vermont artifacts, from a Native American wigwam to a re-creation of the Catamount Tavern (the favorite watering hole of the Green Mountain Boys). Named after the state motto, the award-winning "Freedom and Unity" multimedia exhibit is another highlight. It's

an eloquent, family-friendly exploration of the local desire to balance individual and community needs.

Info: 109 State St
Open Tues.-Sat. 10am-4pm (year round), Sun. 12-4pm (May-Oct.)
Admission $5, $12 for families
Tel. 802-828-2291
www.vermonthistory.org

For all its history, Montpelier has its share of artistic appeal too. The **T.W. Wood Gallery and Art Center** on College Street is one of the state's oldest, most celebrated arts institutions, with a rich, regional-centered collection. The Lost Nation Theater – one of the top companies in the region – and the old time **Savoy cinema** offer prime evening entertainment. One could argue, however, that Montpelier's most artistic creations are generated nightly at the **New England Culinary Institute**. Combine a visit to either theater with a meal at the **Chef's Table**, the institute's flagship eatery, for a memorable evening out.

Info: T.W. Wood Gallery
36 College St

SIGHTS

SIGHTS

Open Tues.-Sun. 12-4pm
Admission free.
Tel. 802-828-8743
www.twwoodgallery.org
Lost Nation Theater
39 Main St
Tel. 802-229-0492
www.lostnationtheater.org
Savoy Theater
26 Main St
Tel. 802-229-0509
www.savoytheater.com
Chef's Table
118 Main St
Tel. 802-229-9202
www.necidining.com

Beyond Montpelier, Waterbury and Stowe, the only other real town of note in the area is **Barre**. Fifteen minutes from Montpelier via Route 302, the "Granite Capital of the World" is defined by its heritage as the center of the region's stone industry. Barre's most fascinating attraction is the **Rock of Ages Visitor Center**, a 50-acre, 600-foot deep quarry that's the world's largest harvester of granite. For a glimpse deep into the Earth, tour its active quarries, then learn about the industry and observe stonecutters at work during the center's self-guided factory tours.

Afterwards, bowl a few frames

on the center's outdoor granite lane or take a walk through the nearby **Hope Cemetery**. One mile north of town on Route 14, the latter is an outdoor sculpture garden of sorts with some of the most impressive stonework you'll ever see, from traditionally-wrought memorials to contemporary tributes shaped like a race car and a soccer ball.

Info: Rock of Ages
560 Graniteville Road
Open Mon.-Sat. 8:30am-5pm, Sun. 10am-5pm May-Oct
Quarry tours $4.50
Tel. 877-225-7626
www.rockofages.com
Hope Cemetery
262 E. Montpelier Rd
Admission free
Tel. 802-476-6245

That may be it for towns, but you can easily spend the rest of your time in the area off the beaten path, driving back roads, wandering trails and indulging an appetite for local goods. The best synthesis of all three leads north from Stowe on **Route 108**. Stop about 11 miles up to hike the **Sterling Pond Trail** (see *the weekend section*), then continue north for some of the

SIGHTS

area's best driving. Pristine and undeveloped, this part of the state offers some of its most subtly majestic scenery, from roadside streams to cloud-streaked swaths of sky.

Continuing another eight miles along Route 108 brings you to its junction with Route 15 and the towns of **Cambridge** and **Jeffersonville**. Charming villages both, they offer, in addition to their scenery, some of Vermont's best local products. Learn how trees are tapped and syrup is made at the family-owned **Vermont Maple Outlet** in Jeffersonville, then cross over to Cambridge via Route 15 to sample the **Boyden Valley Winery's** latest vintages. Based out of a restored red carriage barn, this four generation family farm produces outstanding fruit and dessert wines alongside its flagship Riverbend and Big Barn reds.

Info: Vermont Maple Outlet
3929 Route 15, Jeffersonville
Open daily 9am-5pm
Tel. 800-858-3121
www.vermontmapleoutlet.com
Boyden Valley Winery
Route 104, Cambridge
Open daily 10am-5pm May-
Dec.; Fri.-Sun. 10am-5pm

Jan.-Apr
Tastings $5
Tel. 802-644-8151
www.boydenvalley.com

For nature-generated excitement in this area, consider an **outdoor adventure tour**. The fine folks at **Umiak** lead all kinds of outdoor excursions, from dogsledding to kayaking. many of which are designed for beginners. Their paddling tours on the Lamoille and Winooski Rivers are particularly recommended, as are specialty excursions like moonlight snowshoe treks and the "River and Spirit" tour combining kayaking and a visit to the Boyden Valley Winery.

Info: 849 S. Main St., Stowe

SIGHTS

Tel. 802-253-2317
www.umiak.com

Intrepid outdoor types will also want to devote multiple days to the trails scattered on Stowe's mountainsides. Southeast of the village off Upper Hollow Road, **Stowe Pinnacle** is a relatively short (2.8 miles round trip) yet challenging hike culminating in wide-open views of the surrounding peaks and the Worcester Range. Allow approximately three hours start to finish, and figure on sweating as you make your way up its rocky, forested face. Don't worry – it's worth it.

Serious hikers will also want to consider climbing **Mt. Mansfield**. To undertake this challenging day hike, get on the Long Trail 8.5 miles from Stowe Village on Route 108 or follow the Sunset Ridge Trail from **Underhill State Park**. Both pay off with seriously exhilarating, hard-earned views once you get above the treeline. For further outdoor advice, consult the **Green Mountain Club's** online recommendations at *www.greenmountainclub.org.*

Centrally-located Stowe also offers easy access to at least three other neighboring regions: the Mad River Valley, Burlington, and the Northeast Kingdom, each with its own chapter in this book.

BEST SLEEPS & EATS

STOWE

Stone Hill Inn $$$

With elegant wrought-iron beds and fireside Jacuzzi tubs, Stowe's most romantic luxury inn makes a divine couple's getaway. Get lost in its 10 acres of gardens, trails

and waterfalls, or relax in hammocks, in Adirondack chairs or by the stone fireplace. All nine guest rooms offer high-end luxuries (fine linens, flat screen televisions) and superlative views of the property, as does the window-walled dining room where a gourmet breakfast is served daily by candlelight. *Info: www.stonehillinn.com. Tel. 802-253-6282. 89 Houston Farm Rd. 9 rooms.*

Stowe Mountain Resort $$$

Stowe's prime mountain resort offers a multitude of lodging options, from luxury hotel to inn and condo-style accommodations. With its alpine-chic décor, 21,000-foot day spa and lakeside golf course, the shiny new Stowe Mountain Lodge is by far the most luxurious. The timber and stone exterior belies the lavishness of the guest rooms. Ranging from studios to three-bedroom suites, they include flat screens, bamboo linens, marble baths and private terraces with mountain views. If such luxury is out of your price range, the slopeside Inn at the Mountain is a none too shabby alternative. Smaller, more rustic and more affordable, it offers well-appointed rooms, a heated outdoor pool, clay tennis courts and landscaped grounds. *Info: www.stowe.com. Tel. 888-478-6938. Stowe Mountain Lodge, 7412 Mountain Rd. 139 rooms. Info: www.stowemountainlodge.com. Inn at the Mountain, 5781 Mountain Rd. 33 rooms. Info: www.innatthemountain.com.*

Stoweflake $$$

It's hard to believe this mountain resort and world-class spa started out 45 years ago as a motel. Now a AAA Four Diamond luxury property, Stoweflake offers deluxe accommodations that range from fireplaced guest rooms to suites, townhomes and even a full-size ski house that sleeps ten. The 50,000-square foot spa is just a few years old and features a Hungarian mineral soaking pool and 12-foot high massaging waterfall. Other diversions big and small include Stoweflake's annual hot air balloon festival and the addictive chocolate chip cookies available all over the resort. *Info: www.stoweflake.com. Tel. 802-253-7355. 1746 Mountain Rd. 178 rooms.*

Trapp Family Lodge $$$

The Green Mountains meet the Alps at this Austrian style-chalet that's been owned and operated by the Trapp family (of *Sound of*

Music fame) for over half a century. The 2,400-acre property's perfectly suited to cross country skiing – in fact, it was the country's first Nordic ski center – and you can get happily lost on its countless back-woods trails regardless of season. The Trapp's rustic charm, however, is leavened with plenty of European elegance, from its sparkling dining room to formal gardens and first-class massage facilities. Children's activities are also outstanding. *Info: www.trappfamily.com. Tel. 802-253-8511. 700 Trapp Hill Rd. 96 rooms.*

Green Mountain Inn $$-$$$

This classically-columned red brick inn dates to 1833, and it's managed to retain many of the best features of that period. Afternoon tea is still served in the living room, and a refined yet comfortable ambiance prevails throughout the inn. Warm woods and local watercolor scenes define the décor, and rooms are well-appointed with locally wrought furnishings and canopy beds. A year-round heated pool, fitness center and massage facilities are also provided. *Info: www.greenmountaininn.com. 18 Main St. Tel. 802-253-7301. 107 rooms.*

Mountain Road Resort $$-$$$

More intimate than most, this locally owned, three diamond resort has been a Mountain Road fixture for nearly 50 years. The main lodge terrace invites lounging in summer and marshmallow roasting in winter, and interiors such as the wine bar, library and fireplaced living room are just as comfortable. Four levels of accommodation range from standard rooms to condo suites with gas-powered fireplaces and Jacuzzi tubs. There is an indoor heated pool and outdoor heated spa as well. *Info: www.mountainroadresort.com. Tel. 802-253-4566. 1007 Mountain Rd. 31 rooms.*

Grey Fox Inn & Resort $$

Next to the Stowe Recreation Path, the Grey Fox is a fine mid-range lodging option with an enviable connection to the adjoining Dutch Pancake Café breakfast spot. Carriage house rooms are the most affordable; the Mountain View Manor has the best amenities and the best views; and traditional and deluxe quarters in the main inn split the difference. Shared facilities include multiple swimming pools, a fireplaced sitting room and a recently renovated pub and lounge. *Info: www.stowegreyfoxinn.com. Tel. 802-253-8344. 990 Mountain Rd. 41 rooms.*

Stowehof Inn & Resort $$

A fine compromise between an inn and a resort, Stowehof comfortably blends interior co-ziness (fireplaced nooks, full break-fast) with top-notch facilities (two pools, indoor and outdoor hot tubs

and a sauna). Accommodations range from basic traditional rooms to premier Pinnacle rooms with canopy beds, floor-to-ceiling windows and vaulted ceilings. Package options involving sleigh rides and on-premises fine dining are also worth considering. *Info: www.stowehofinn.com. Tel. 800-932-7136. 434 Edson Hill Rd. 46 rooms.*

Ye Olde England Inne $$

Old England meets New England at this vintage inn that's a blend of Vermont farmhouse and Tudor-style architecture. The 150-year old main inn has a flagstone fireplace, Laura Ashley décor and guest rooms such as the Cranford (with cherry canopy bed and whirlpool tub) and the Cumbria (with English wardrobe and views of Mount Mansfield). Luxury suites are situated in the Bluff House, and a number of cottages are spread over the eight-acre property. Both the welcoming owners and the inn's award-winning gastropub add British character. *Info: www.englandinn.com. Tel. 802-253-7558. 433 Mountain Rd. 30 rooms.*

Golden Eagle $-$$

Within walking distance of the town center, this 80-acre, family-owned complex offers far more amenities than the average hotel at prices much lower than Stowe's fancier resorts. A popular value option for families, its basic guest rooms (some suites, many with fireplace) are enhanced by the nice grounds and nature trails, an indoor pool and a spa and fitness center. A range of supervised programs are offered for children. *Info: www.goldeneagleresort.com. Tel. 802-253-4811. 511 Mountain Ave. 89 rooms.*

Smuggler's Notch Inn $-$$

Just over the Notch and close to the Smuggler's Notch Resort, this porch-fronted inn on Route 108 occupies a historic 1790 building that was completely renovated just a few years ago. Well-appointed guest rooms are furnished with locally handmade lamps, and some have Jacuzzis and four-poster beds. A tavern, bakery and intimate dining room are also on the premises. *Info: www.smuggsinn.com. Tel. 802-644-6607. 55 Church St., Jeffersonville. 11 rooms.*

Timberholm Country B&B $-$$

Rich pine interiors and a beautiful fieldstone fireplace give the Timberholm a classic mountain charm. The long red house was one of Stowe's first lodges, and a stay here – whether in the close-quartered Cabin room or the large corner Timber room with vintage quilt and Tiffany lamp – remains an old-fashioned value. The property's gardens and woods are ideal for birding, and the back deck looks out on the surrounding mountains. *Info: www.timberholm.com. Tel. 802-253-7603. 452 Cottage Club Rd. 10 rooms.*

Solstice $$$

Whether you're seated in the 110-seat, window-walled dining room or on the open-air deck, the views of Spruce Peak here are priceless – and good thing, as the Stowe Mountain Lodge's rustically ritzy restaurant is otherwise among the most expensive in the area. Dine on deluxe entrees such as Champlain rabbit and dry aged Vermont tenderloin, or choose the "money is no object" four or seven-course tasting menus. Breakfast features an interactive chef station, and custom pottery, hand-carved furniture and an open kitchen add further ambiance. *Info: Stowe Mountain Lodge, 7412 Mountain Rd. Tel. 802-760-4735. Breakfast, lunch and dinner daily. www.stowemountainlodge.com.*

Trapp Family Lodge $$$

The main dining room of the Trapp Family resort epitomizes European elegance. Classical music and candelight complement the serene mountain views outside as well as the classy Continental cuisine served within. From wiener schnitzel to venison, the dinner menu merges the best of Austrian and New England traditions, and can be ordered *prix fixe* or à la carte. Reservations and appropriate attire are required. *Info: 700 Trapp Hill Rd. Tel. 800-826-7000. Breakfast and dinner daily. Lunch daily in Austrian Tea Room. Dinner reservations required. www.trappfamily.com.*

Blue Moon Café $$-$$$

The menu rotates weekly at this inviting, wood-beamed dining room just off Mountain Road. Appetizers (goat cheese and bitter greens, oysters on the half shell) match well with the *Wine Spectator*-recognized wine list, and house specialties include rack of lamb and grilled chicken with spiced apples and sweet potatoes. Small plate specials during the week and build your own salad options add an extra dose of creativity and affordability. *Info: 35 School St. Tel. 802-253-7006. Dinner daily. www.bluemoonstowe.com.*

Cliff House $$-$$$

On the crest of Mount Mansfield at the summit of the Stowe gondola, the chalet-style Cliff House affords stunning mountain views through its floor-to-ceiling windows. The traditional cuisine has a local flavor, and "high altitude" dinner packages (complete with gondola ride and hot cider) are offered on select Saturday evenings. *Info: 5781 Mountain Rd. Tel. 802-253-3665. Lunch daily. www.stowe.com/activities/dining.*

Mr. Pickwick's $$-$$$

Dickens would be pleased by the authenticity of this British gastropub housed in the Ye Olde England Inne. The stone-arched interior and brew-happy enthusiasm mesh well with the kitchen's gourmet takes on traditional Anglo fare (beef Wellington, bangers and mash). The signature oyster-steak-kidney pie pairs best with the Ayinger Celebrator – though most any of the pub's 150+ brews will do. *Info: 433 Mountain Rd. Tel. 802-253-7558. Breakfast, lunch and dinner daily. www.mrpickwicks.com.*

158 Main $$

Convenient to Smugglers Notch and the Boyden Valley winery, Jeffersonville's best restaurant offers quaint ambiance and quality fare morning, noon and night. Comfort food (beef stew, French bread pizzas) co-exists happily alongside steaks and seafood on the dinner menu while the bakery and the variety of Benedict breakfast sandwiches make this Main Street institution an inspired breakfast stop as well. *Info: 158 Main St., Jeffersonville. Tel. 802-644-8100. Breakfast, lunch and dinner Tues.-Sun. www.158main.com.*

Dutch Pancake Café $$
Pannekoeken – the Dutch hybrid of the pancake and the crepe – rules the menu at this breakfast-time café next to the Grey Fox Inn. A foot in diameter, they come in over 80 sweet or savory varieties. *Info: 990 Mountain Rd. Tel. 802-253-8921. Breakfast and brunch daily. www.stowegreyfoxinn.com.*

Piecasso $$
Run by a second generation Sicilian, this inviting pizzeria is as close to New York style as Stowe gets. The creatively-named pies (vegetarian Tree Hugger, meat covered Carcass) are hand-tossed and hearth-baked, and lasagna, sandwiches and seasonal soups are also served. The neon-lit bar often offers live music and is a popular après-ski destination. *Info: 1899 Mountain Rd. Tel. 802-253-4411. Lunch and dinner daily. www.piecasso.com.*

Red Basil $$
Serious house specials like sirloin, shrimp teriyaki and the "swimming" (soft shell crab and duck in red curry) lure adventurous diners to Stowe's only Thai restaurant. A range of soups and noodle and curry dishes make it a prime lunch spot as well. *Info: 294 Mountain Rd. Tel. 802-253-4478. Lunch and dinner daily. www.theredbasil.com.*

The Bee's Knees $-$$
Fifteen minutes from Stowe in small yet vibrant Morrisville, this community café is known as the "town's living room" on account of its close-knit coziness (couches, tables, art, games) and warm local cuisine. Pot pies, salads and cre-

ative vegetarian options are standout fare and, combined with a selection of local beers and live music most nights, are leading to increased regional buzz. *Info: 82 Lower Main St., Morrisville. Tel. 802-888-7889. Breakfast, lunch and dinner Tues.-Sun. www.thebeesknees-vt.com.*

The Shed $

The burgers are marinated in beer, and the beer sampler is served in a ski at this brewpub that's a favorite of both families and the après-ski crowd. Ribs and stacked nacho plates pair well with the crisp Mountain Ale that is also available in growlers to go. *Info: 1859 Mountain Rd. Tel. 802-253-4364. Lunch and dinner daily.*

MONTPELIER
The Inn at Montpelier $$-$$$

Two Federal style houses – including one of the oldest frame

houses in Vermont – exude the charm and sense of history one would expect of Montpelier's best inn. Distinctive bed frames and antique furniture (Chippendale desks, Queen Anne chairs) are standard décor, and deluxe rooms add custom four-poster beds and fireplaces. If that's not enough warmth for you, the common areas offer five additional fireplaces. *Info: www.innatmontpelier.com. 147 Main St. Tel. 802-223-2727. 19 rooms.*

Betsy's B&B $-$$

This affordable bed and breakfast is close to the State House and offers a dozen rooms spread across two 19th century Victorian homes. All come with private bath and period décor, and some have sitting rooms and kitchens. Breakfast is included, and common areas (garden, fireplaced parlor) are welcoming. *Info: www.central-vt.com/web/betsybb. 74 E. State St. Tel. 802-229-0466. 12 rooms.*

SLEEPS & EATS

Restaurant Phoebe $$-$$$

Just down the street from the State House, this chef-owned, 48-seat bistro serves creative American cuisine in a light, high-ceilinged dining room with open kitchen. Entrees range from squash ravioli to sweetbreads and surf and turf, and the lunchtime spread of burgers and panini sandwiches is popular with politicos and tourists alike. *Info: 52 State St. Tel. 802-262-3500. Lunch Mon.-Fri, dinner Tues.-Sat. www.restaurantphoebe.com.*

Main Street Grill & Bar $$

The Montpelier-based New England Culinary Institute runs this charming bistro (and the La Brioche bakery café down the street) as a teaching restaurant. Dine on classic New England dishes (cider braised pork, stuffed chicken) as interpreted by the celebrity chefs of tomorrow, or simply stop by for

bar fare (along with live music on Tuesdays) or the fabulous Sunday brunch. *Info: 118 Main St. Tel. 802-223-3188. Lunch and dinner Tues.-Sun. www.necidining.com.*

Kismet $-$$

Where else but Vermont can you order a Philly cheese steak and a dandelion latte as part of the same meal? It's kismet for sure – especially in this colorful, daytime-only restaurant that also specializes in breakfast crepes and creative sandwiches that would be guilty pleasures if they weren't made with local, organic, primarily healthful ingredients. *Info: 207 Barre St. Tel. 802-223-8646. Breakfast and lunch Wed.-Sun. www.kismetkitchen.com.*

That's Life Soup $

Arts and Crafts décor and authentically old-school soups make That's Life more an exclamation than a sigh of resignation. Meat and vegetarian soups are both flavorful and filling, and the cheesecake is a local treasure. *Info: 41 Elm St. Tel. 802-223-5333. Lunch and dinner Mon.-Fri.*

Positive Pie $

This funky Plainfield pizzeria recently opened a more urbane outpost-lounge in Montpelier. Fresh-made pastas complement the New York style pies, and the color-lit interior is as inviting for late night music and dancing as for a quick beer and slice. *Info: 22 State St., Montpelier and 69 Main St., Plainfield. Lunch and dinner daily. Tel. 802-229-0453. www.positivepie.com.*

WATERBURY
Hen of the Wood $$$

How serendipitous to think that the Waterbury Feed Company's 19th century grist mill would become home to one of Vermont's prime foodie destinations in the 21st. Whether you dine next to the stone-filled stream in summer or on the candlelit balcony in winter, you'll find the ambiance – and the locally informed cuisine – second to none. The frequently-changing menu includes such delicacies as sheep's milk gnocchi, short ribs and seared sea scallops as well as an exclusively local cheese plate and an exclusively North American wine list. A tasting menu is offered on weeknights. *Info: 92 Stowe St., Waterbury. Tel. 802-244-7300. Dinner Mon.-Sat. www.henofthewood.com.*

The Alchemist $$

The best brewpub in a region full of them melds malt, hops and a hearty menu into one of Vermont's most casually memorable dining experiences. Housed in what was once the Waterbury Post Office, it delivers seven house-made ales nightly, but one need not love beer to fall under the Alchemist's spell. Its imaginative pub fare and desserts – including a decadent maple porter pudding cake – delight teetotalers and beer geeks alike. *Info: 23 S. Main St. Tel. 802-244-4120. Dinner daily.* www.alchemistbeer.com.

Waterbury Wings $
There are nearly as many wing sauces (23) as draft beers (30) at Waterbury's much-lauded wing and tap room. Try novel varieties such as honey habanero, which melds sweet with heat. All come with traditional carrot, celery and blue cheese accompaniment. *Info: 1 S. Main St. Tel. 802-244-7827. Lunch and dinner daily.* www.waterburywings.com.

BEST SHOPPING

Stowe Area
Stowe's best shopping is clustered along **Main Street** and **Mountain Road**. All told, the village has more than 45 shops specializing in art, jewelry, clothing, crafts and more. The **Stowe Mercantile country store** on Main Street stocks a little bit of everything, as does the arts and clothing-centered **Stowe Craft Gallery and Design Center** (*55 Mountain Rd.*) The **Sunday farmers' market** along Mountain Road is also a good place to find handcrafted souvenirs. Sport-centered shopping can be found all along Mountaain Road as well. **Pinnacle Ski and Sports** (*3391 Mountain Rd.*) and the **Nordic Barn** (*4081 Mountain Rd.*) are both reliable options.

For further suggestions, visit www.gostowe.com.

Waterbury has abundant, tourist-centered shopping along **Waterbury-Stowe Road/Route 100**, including the **Ben & Jerry's gift shop**; the **Cabot Cheese Annex**; and the **Cold Hollow Cider Mill**'s vast selection of Vermont products and foodstuffs. Also on Route 100, the **Vermont Teddy Bear Company shop** is a must-stop for children while the **Ziemke Glassblowing Studio** provides a fascinating glimpse into an unheralded art form. For more information on shopping in the area, visit www.waterbury.org.

SHOPPING

Montpelier
With a number of bookstores, gift shops and galleries, Montpelier's lively, compact downtown is an underrated shopping destination. **Bear**

Pond Books, Rivendell Books and the **Artisans Hand craft shop** are all within a couple of blocks on picturesque Main Street, and **Onion River Sports** (*20 Langdon St.*) is one of the better outdoor outfitters in the area. For more information, visit *www.montpelier-vt.org.*

BEST NIGHTLIFE & ENTERTAINMENT

Stowe Area
Stowe offers a lively nightlife scene, with plenty of après-ski action at bars and nightclubs alike. **The Shed** brewpub (*1859 Mountain Rd., Tel. 802-253-4765*) offers house-brewed ales in a boisterous yet family-friendly atmosphere; **Piecasso** (*1899 Mountain Rd., Tel. 802-253-4411*) has the town's best pizza and live music; and the **Rusty Nail** (*1190 Mountain Rd., Tel. 802-253-6245*) is the most party-conducive with dancing, DJs and a "black diamond" martini bar. **The Brewski** on Route 108 in Jeffersonville (*Tel. 802-644-6366*) is the best après-ski op-

tion near Smuggler's Notch. Local drafts, pool tables and friendly owner-bartenders distinguish it from the rest of the roadside watering holes. For the very best brews in the area – and perhaps in all of Vermont – you'll have to travel to Waterbury, home of the magical **Alchemist** brewpub (*23 Main St, Tel. 802-244-4120*).

Though bars and restaurants represent the majority of nightlife, Stowe does have an active theater scene, particularly in summer when the **Stowe Theatre Guild** (*67 Main St., Tel. 802-253-3961*) schedule takes off. **Stowe Per-**

NIGHTLIFE & ENTERTAINMENT

forming Arts (*Tel. 802-253-7792, www.stowearts.com*) is the leading summer concert presenter, and you can catch a film any time of year at the three-screen **cinemaplex** on Mountain Road (*Tel. 802-253-4678*).

Montpelier

Popular late-night hangouts in Montpelier include the **Black Door pub** (*44 Main St., Tel. 802-223-7070*) and **Positive Pie's** neon-lit lounge-pizzeria (*22 State St., Tel. 802-229-0453*). Theater options abound, from **Lost Nation** **Theater's** performances at the **City Hall Arts Center** (*39 Main St., Tel. 802-229-0492*) to **Unadilla Theatre's** summer performances in an old barn just northeast of Montpelier in Marshfield (*501 Blachly Rd., Tel. 802-456-8968*). The multi-screen **Capitol Theater** (*93 State St., Tel. 802-229-0343*) shows first-run movies, and the **Savoy Theater** (*26 Main St., Tel. 802-229-0509*) – site of the **Green Mountain Film Festival** every March – screens classic and art-house fare nightly in its century-old theater across from City Hall.

BEST SPORTS & RECREATION

Stowe Area

With numerous resorts, backwoods trails and a generous annual snowfall, Stowe is rightly famous as a skier's paradise. From winding, old-fashioned trails to the Spruce Peak and Toll House beginner slopes to the "Front Four" double diamond trails, **Stowe Mountain Resort** (*off Route 108/, www.stowe.com*) has 48 trails of appealing variety. Cross country skiing is nearly as popular. The **Trapp Family Lodge** (*700 Trapp Hill Rd.,* *www.trappfamily.com*) and the **Edson Hill Nordic Center** (*1500 Edson Hill Rd., www.edsonhillmanor.com*) provide access to miles of groomed trails, and many

STOWE TROLLEY

The free **Mountain Road Shuttle** runs every half-hour from town to the slopes. It stops at various inns along the way and is also a great way to tour the town in summer. *Info: Schedules are available at www.gmtaride.org.*

other inns have grounds well-suited to this purpose as well. When booking a room, inquire about ski packages that incorporate lodging with trail access or lift tickets.

Consistently less crowded than Stowe, the **Smugglers' Notch Resort** (*4323 Route 108, Tel. 800-419-4615, www.smuggs.com*) in Jeffersonville supports a range of winter activities (snow tubing, ice skating, dogsledding) on three mountains along with superior ski and snowboarding terrain for all abilities. While the "Black Hole" is notorious as the only triple black diamond

trail on the east coast, Smuggs is also widely considered to be Vermont's top family resort, as it offers award-winning children's programs, child care and the country's only ski instruction program for toddlers.

As the seasons change, so does Stowe's range of outdoor activity. Come summer, hiking, biking, fishing and swimming are all popular pastimes. Many inns and hotels have tennis courts, and the recent addition of the Stowe Mountain Club at **Stowe Mountain Resort** (*Tel. 802-253-3000*) has made the area even more of a hotbed for golf. The resort now has 36 holes of championship-caliber golf, including the historic Stowe Country Club links that are the home base of the Vermont Golf Academy. The **Farm Resort and Golf Course** (*326 Laporte Rd., Morrisville, Tel. 802-888-3535*) north of Stowe is an outstanding nine-hole course, and there are another dozen courses within an hour's drive.

The mountains around Stowe offer some of the very best hiking in the state. **Mount Mansfield** is the most thrilling option. Four major trails lead to its summit; the Cliff and Profanity Trails are the most difficult and make the Long and Haselton Trails seem mild in comparison. Other top treks in the area include the Sterling Pond and Stowe Pinnacle Trails; directions and more information on both can be found in the Stowe itinerary section. The most accessible trail in town is the **Stowe Recreation Path**, a 5.5-mile all-purpose track extending from the village to the covered bridge on Mountain Road. It's equally well-suited to walking, biking and cross country skiing.

There's no shortage of mountains, trails and waterways throughout the surrounding area either. The Catamount and Long Trails both wend their way around Stowe, and swimming holes pop up at many a mountain road turn-off. With a small beach and photogenic cascades, **Jeff Falls** in Jeffersonville (south of town off Route 108) is one of the best. For a bona fide lake experience, head to **Lake Elmore** off Route 12 (*Tel. 802-888-2982*). Known as the "Beauty Spot of Vermont," it's surrounded by 36 miles of

CATAMOUNT TRAIL

North America's longest cross-country trail is 300 miles long and runs the length of the state. Touring centers can be found all along the trail, and many resorts' facilities link up with it too. For more information on Nordic skiing and snowshoeing on the trail, call the **Catamount Trail Association.** *Info: Tel. 802-864-5794, www.catamounttrail.org.*

state parkland and offers beach access, hiking trails and high-quality camping facilities.

To the south of Stowe off Route 100, **Waterbury Reservoir State Park** (*Tel. 802-244-1226*)provides swimming, boating and nature trails that run through the Mount Mansfield State Forest. Also in Waterbury off Route 2, **Little River State Park** (*Tel. 802-244-7103*) is a great camping spot that also offers boating and picturesque, low-intensity terrain for hiking. If you're looking for guidance or a little adventure, consider an **Umiak adventure tour.** The

SPORTS & RECREATION

area's leading outdoor outfitter leads river trips and snowshoeing and dog sledding and expeditions and rents a wide range of equipment at its retail store in Stowe (*849 S. Main St., Tel. 802-253-2317*).

Montpelier
Bike paths run in and out of Montpelier, and you can rent a cycle – and plenty of other equipment too – at **Onion**

River Sports on Langdon Street (*Tel. 802-229-9409*). The **Winooski River** runs past town and is a popular choice for canoeing and kayaking. North Branch and Hubbard parks are prime areas for skiing and hiking, and the trails around the Vermont Institute of Natural Science's **North Branch Nature Center** (*713 Elm St., Tel. 802-229-6206*) are particularly ideal territory for birding and wildlife spotting.

8. BURLINGTON & NORTHWEST VERMONT

HIGHLIGHTS

▲ Burlington/UVM Campus

▲ Shelburne Museum & Farms

▲ Winooski/Essex Junction

▲ Lake Champlain

▲ Vermont Teddy Bear/Minor League Baseball

INTRO

With its mountain-framed waterfront and youthful, laid-back attitude, **Burlington** is New England's answer to the Pacific Northwest. Set on the scenic shores of **Lake Champlain**, Vermont's largest city is a sort of small-scale Seattle, beautiful, cosmopolitan and as comfortable outdoors as in. Whether you're a shopper or a sailor, you're sure to enjoy Burlington's range of activities and breezy lakeside vibe. An ideal base for exploring **northern Vermont**, the city also offers easy access to the region's considerable natural wonders, from the lake islands to the nearby mountains of Stowe.

COORDINATES

Burlington sits on the edge of **Lake Champlain** and lies at the intersection of **Rt. 7, Rt. 2/1-89**, and **Rt. 15**. From New York State, you can take a ferry across the lake from **Port Kent** directly into Burlington, or from **Essex** to Charlotte, Vermont.

SIGHTS

BURLINGTON SIGHTS IN A DAY

Start your day in Burlington in the city's most dynamic public space – the **Church Street Marketplace** (*see photo on previous page*). A "Great American Main Street" according to the National Trust for Historic Preservation, this charming, pedestrian-only thoroughfare offers prime shopping and dining options as well as Burlington's best people watching. Street vendors, college students, dogs, families out shopping – all are represented along Church Street's leafy, brick-paved blocks. Soak in the atmosphere from a park bench, perhaps with a coffee from Uncommon Grounds, or stroll past its flags, fountain and flagship retailers for one of the prettiest urban shopping experiences in America.

Info: Uncommon Grounds
42 Church St
Tel. 802-865-6227
www.ugvermont.com

From Church Street you can branch off to explore the rest of downtown. Make your way along College, Main and Pearl Streets past more shops and restaurants, including **Bove's** classic Italian diner (*see Best*

SIGHTS

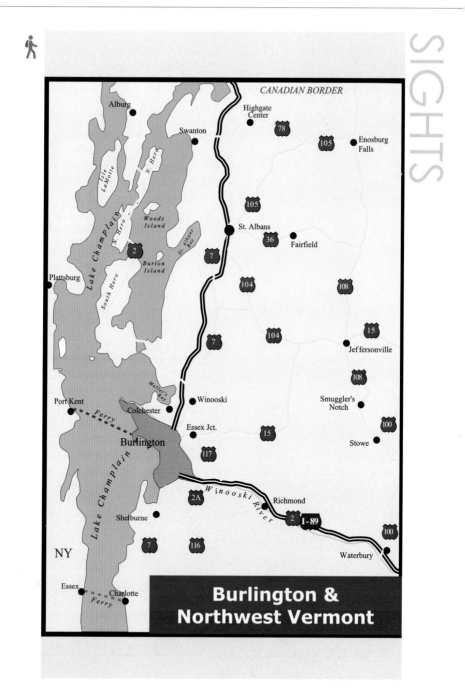

Burlington & Northwest Vermont

SIGHTS

Sleeps & Eats) then continue due west until you reach the waterfront.

Just five minutes from the town center, **Lake Champlain** would seem like a mirage if it wasn't so irrefutably large. The country's sixth most substantial body of fresh water (only the Great Lakes are bigger), Champlain exerts a placid yet powerful presence on the region. Seen from above from Battery Park (at the intersection of Pearl and Battery Streets) and along the walkway that follows Battery Street south, it's particularly beautiful, its faraway depths and mountain-fringed shoreline

scuffed with clouds and sea-dream haze.

Closer to shore, take an early afternoon ramble through Burlington's **Waterfront Park**. A boardwalk promenade and bike path follows the shoreline, making it a favorite destination for lounging locals and workout warriors alike. Consider returning around dusk, as this is a great place to catch a sunset.

At the southern edge of Waterfront Park, at its intersection with College Street, is **ECHO**, Burlington's shiny, glass-encased **aquarium and science center**. ECHO stands for "Ecology, Culture, History and Opportunity," and its chambers contain a little on each as they pertain to Lake Champlain. Exhibits for kids, such as the tide pool touch tank, are strengths, as is the Awesome Forces Theater, a visual tour-de-force that condenses Earth's 4.5-billion year odyssey into a series of action-packed, elemental explosions. Interactive and live animal exhibits throughout the museum spotlight over 70 local species, from fish to amphibians to reptiles. Many of them surface for daily public feedings, though the lake's most notorious creature, Champ the sea monster, appears only in legend.

Info: *1 College St*
Open daily 10am-5pm
Admission $9.50, children $7
Tel. 877-324-6386
www.echovermont.org

Burlington remains vibrant into the evening. The **American Flatbread** restaurant and brewpub near the center of town (*see Best Sleeps & Eats*) is the most casually delicious culinary hotspot in a town that's full of them. Famous for its wood-fired thin crust pizza, it's popular with locals, which means you'll likely have to wait for a table (no reservations), but that's no matter when you can saddle up to the hearthside bar for a house-made Zero Gravity beer.

Linger here into the night, or else imbibe some culture right around the corner at the historic **Flynn Center**. Once a vaudeville house, today's Flynn is an art deco masterpiece of a theater that plays host to Broadway hits, dance groups and the Vermont Symphony Orchestra.

Info: *153 Main St*
Tel. 802-863-5966.
www.flynncenter.org

A WEEKEND IN THE BURLINGTON AREA

If you arrive early enough on Friday night, start the weekend in style with a sneak preview of the Church Street Marketplace. With a number of excellent restaurants, wine bars and coffee shops, it's an al fresco hotbed in summer and festively illuminated in winter.

You can structure your Saturday in Burlington pretty much as outlined in the one-day plan, though be sure to incorporate the town's lively **Farmers' Market** into your morning plan. More craft-centric than many markets, it's a great place to find homemade local goods from jewelry to soaps. Fresh foods and flowers are in abundance too, and the people watching – live musicians, dogs, kids everywhere – is just as refreshing.

Info: *City Hall Park*

SIGHTS

149 Church St
Open Sat. 8:30am-2pm, May-Oct. Indoor market at Memorial Auditorium third Sat. of every month, 10am-2pm in off season
Tel. 888-889-8188
www.burlingtonfarmersmarket.org

Given the area's wealth of attractions and natural beauty, you'd expect the plan for Sunday to involve a compromise between culture or the outdoors. Fortunately Vermont's marquee arts attraction, the **Shelburne Museum**, is the perfect union of the two and just nine miles south of Burlington via Route 7.

Sensational and sprawling enough to require the better part of a day, the Shelburne is spread across 45 acres of vintage Vermont countryside. Its gardens, hills and dales, however, are dotted with some of the most beautiful buildings and historic relics you'll ever see. Rather than restrict herself to artwork, Electra Havemeyer Webb, the museum's founder, collected and installed all manner of finds here, including a barn, a train, a carousel, a covered bridge, a Quaker meeting house and a number of subtly stunning stone cottages straight out of the 18th and 19th centuries.

Acting as collections within collections, each of these structures reveals even more fascinating works inside. Filled with folk art, impressionist paintings and examples of period architecture and design, room after room at the Shelburne astounds with remarkable specimens (150,000 objects in all) that blend artistry with industry and, ultimately, transmit a palpably vital picture of the American people. More interactive than a technology exhibit and as authentically American as anything in Washington, D.C., the Shelburne attracts people of all ages and interests. Exhibits involving quilts, circus

SIGHTS

toys and the tourable Ticonderoga steamship have particularly wide ranging appeal.

Plan to arrive at the Shelburne by late morning and stay till late afternoon. It's just that big, that varied and that interesting. Even if you don't linger over every glint and texture (and here's where I should thank my companions again for their patience), you'll still want to spend a hard minimum of three or four hours roaming the grounds, admiring everything from the picturesque village setting to the Shelburne's impeccable, impossibly colored flower beds.

*Info: Route 7, Shelburne
Open daily 10am-5pm mid-May to late Oct
Admission $20 (valid for 2 days), $10 after 3pm, $10 for children
Tel. 802-985-3346
www.shelburnemuseum.org*

ALTERNATIVE PLAN

For an alternate take on the way things were, spend your Sunday at **Shelburne Farms**. A 1,400-acre working farm less than three miles from the Shelburne Museum, this National Historic Landmark not only preserves but continues to implement traditional farming customs. Demonstrations take place May through October,

but the farm's eight miles of walking trails make great strolling year round. For a do-it-all approach to the Shelburne area, stop at the farm first, then pay an abbreviated homage to the Shelburne Museum after 3 pm, when admission is reduced to $10. ***Info:** 1611 Harbor Rd., Shelburne. Open daily 10 am-4 pm. Farmyard open May-Oct. Admission $6, $4 for children. Tel. 802-985-8686. www.shelburnefarms.org.*

SIGHTS

Before heading home, take a peek at the **Shelburne Village Historic District**. The small yet well preserved stretch of Route 7 features a number of handsome 19th century buildings as well as antique stores and charming shops such as **Village Wine and Coffee**. Cap your visit with a cappuccino or, better yet, with an early dinner at the **Bearded Frog**, a classy yet cozy bistro in the Shelburne Inn (see *Best Sleeps & Eats*).

Info: Village Wine and Coffee
5288 Shelburne Rd
Tel. 802-985-8922
www.villagewineandcoffee.com

A WEEK IN NORTHWEST VERMONT

From cultural attractions to the outdoors, Greater Burlington offers more than enough activities to keep you busy for an entire week. Consider dividing your time in thirds – say, two town-centered days focused on shopping and culture; two days outdoors, particularly on the lake; and two days devoted to Shelburne and the attractions along Route 7, including Shelburne Farms and the Shelburne Museum.

With two solid days in downtown Burlington, you'll be able to spend some extra time at must-see destinations like the Church Street Marketplace and ECHO aquarium while also experiencing some of the city's more overlooked attractions. The **Robert Hull Fleming Museum** on the University of Vermont campus is one such treasure. Home to the state's largest collection of art and anthropology, its galleries are filled with over 20,000 objects from around the globe, from Native American masks to an Egyptian mummy.

Info: 61 Colchester Ave
Open Tues., Thurs.-Fri. 9am-4pm, Wed. 9am-8pm, Sat.-Sun. 1-5pm May-Aug.; Tues.-Fri. 12-4pm, Sat.-Sun. 1-5pm Sept.-Apr
Admission $5
Tel. 802-656-2090
www.uvm.edu/~fleming

Also consider an extended wander around the **UVM campus** while you're here. New England's fifth oldest college offers an assortment of attractions, from sprawling green lawns to handsome 18th century buildings, and its men's and women's athletic teams – known as the Catamounts – field competitive squads in a number of NCAA sports, from basketball to ice hockey.

Info: *UVM Athletic Dept Patrick Gymnasium, Room 209 Tel. 802-656-4410 www.uvm.edu/~sportspr*

If art's more your thing, spend an afternoon immersed in Burlington's casual yet hip gallery scene. **First Friday art walks** showcase it at its most festive, though you can peruse **local crafts** at centers such as **Frog Hollow** and **Pine Street Art Works** any time you like. **Burlington City Arts** (**BCA** – *see photo below*) is your best source for community-centered work, from open studios and artists' talks to contemporary exhibitions in the Firehouse Gallery. The free *Seven Days* newspaper is a great resource for arts happenings from concerts to gallery openings.

Info: *Frog Hollow 85 Church St. & 250 Main St Tel. 802-863-6458 www.froghollow.org Pine Street Art Works 404 Pine St Tel. 802-863-8100 www.pinestreetartworks.com BCA 135 Church St Tel. 802-865-7166 www.burlingtoncityarts.com*

If you want to tack on a little small-town time, visit Burlington's sister village of **Winooski** just a few minutes away on the opposite side of the Winooski River. Its small yet lively downtown features a handful of boutiques, a music venue and two great dining options on Main Street: **Tiny Thai** for delicious lunch specials and **Sneakers** for café fare and one of the area's top brunches (*see Best Sleeps & Eats*).

SIGHTS

SEVEN DAYS IN BURLINGTON

The **Seven Days** weekly newspaper is full of arts and culture listings, including gallery openings, concerts, movie times and more. Pick up the free publication at newsstands and coffeeshops around town. *Info*: *www.7dvt.com.*

Other towns of note in the area include **Essex Junction** – known for its **outlet shopping** – and **Jericho**, a blink-and-you-might-miss-it town seven miles east of Essex that's home to two of Vermont's best small town tourist gems: the exquisite little **Snowflake Bentley museum**, with its old mill setting and enchanting collection of snowflakes photographed through a microscope; and **Joe's Snack Bar**, a roadside burger shack that's been a locally owned legend for nearly 60 years (*see Best Sleeps & Eats*).

Info: Snowflake Bentley Museum
68 Route 15
Open Mon.-Sat. 10am-5pm, Sun. 11:30am-4pm, mid-March-Dec; closed Mon.-Tues.& Thurs. Jan.-mid March
Admission free

Tel. 802-899-1739
www.snowflakebentley.com

Also worth the short drive out of town is the **Ethan Allen Homestead** a couple of miles north of Burlington off Route 127. Vermont's first celebrity, Allen led the famous Green Mountain Boys through the Revolutionary War period before living his final years in this restored colonial farmhouse. Today the property includes multimedia displays, a re-created tavern and riverside walking trails.

Info: Off Route 127 North House open Mon.-Sat. 10am-5pm, Sun. 1-5pm mid-May-mid-Oct
Admission $5
Park open year round
Admission free
Tel. 802-865-4556
www.ethanallenhomestead.org

Your number one stop outside Burlington, however, must be **Shelburne**. This small yet historic village less than 15 minutes from the city is home to two of Vermont's top cultural attractions, and you'll need two days to see them both properly. You'll want to devote the better part of a day to touring the one-of-a-kind

SIGHTS

Shelburne Museum, and **Shelburne Farms** also merits an extended visit (*see photo at right*). My weekend plan will give you details on both of these must-see destinations. To soak in the full Shelburne experience and reduce your back and forth time, consider an overnight stay at the **Inn at Shelburne Farms** or a nearby bed and breakfast like the **Heart of the Village Inn** (*see Best Sleeps & Eats*).

A trip to Shelburne goes nicely with a food or drink factory tour on Burlington's southern outskirts. The **Magic Hat Brewery** serves up enchanting, foam-capped beers, including its flagship #9 ale, at its factory store in South Burlington. Guided tours of the newly expanded brewery run Thursday through Saturday, though you can take a self-guided peek and try samples Monday through Saturday at the Artifactory.

Info: 5 Bartlett Bay Rd., S. Burlington
Artifactory open Mon.-Sat. 10am-6pm, Sun. 12-5pm.

Tours Thurs.-Fri. 3-5pm, Sat. 12-3pm
Admission free
Tel. 802-658-2739
www.magichat.net

The region's top chocolatier, **Lake Champlain Chocolates**, also has a factory here. Free tours are offered weekdays at the Pine Street factory just a few minutes' drive from downtown, or you can opt for the Saturday fudge-making demonstrations at the company's Church Street Marketplace location. You'll want to try these artisanal bonbons that are routinely recognized among New England's best.

Info: 750 Pine St
Store and café open Mon.-Sat. 9am-6pm, Sun. 12-5pm.
Tours Mon.-Fri. 9am-2pm.
Admission free
Tel. 802-864-1808
www.lakechamplainchocolates.com

SIGHTS

You should be able to take in most all of these attractions and still have more than one day to devote to the outdoors. In milder months, a day at Burlington's **lakeside beaches** should be your first priority. With its supervised swim area, kayak rentals and picnic pavilion, **North Beach** – located at the end of Institute Road off North Avenue just off the Burlington Bike Path – is the biggest and most popular option. **Oakledge Park**, on Burlington's south side at the end of Flynn Avenue, is the most naturally blessed. With flat rocks made for sunning and small cliffs made for jumping, it's pure paradise whether you plan to frolic in the lake or simply read alongside it. On clear days when the sun glints off the water and the mountains, Oakledge offers some of Burlington's best scenery too. Sunsets here are not to be missed.

Info: Burlington Dept. of Parks & Recreation
Tel. 802-864-0123
Beaches open late May through Labor Day
www.enjoyburlington.com

Much more than a great view, Lake Champlain also offers unparalleled opportunities for getting out on the water. Scuba divers embrace the depths of the lake's **Underwater Historic Preserve**, which is home to eight 19th century wrecks, hundreds of fish and plants and one of the world's oldest coral reefs. You can also sail Champlain's shores, either with a boat rental from the **Community Sailing Center** or in classic cruise ship style aboard the **Spirit of Ethan Allen III**. And in the event you were torn over whether to spend your vacation in Burlington or the Bahamas, you'll find the perfect compromise in a luxury, multi-day cruise aboard the **Vermont Moonlight Lady**.

Info: Community Sailing Center
1 Lake St
Tel. 802-864-2499
www.communitysailingcenter.org.
Spirit of Ethan Allen III
Tel. 802-862-8300
www.soea.com
Vermont Moonlight Lady
Boats depart from Burlington Boathouse, 1 College St.
Tel. 802-863-3350
www.vermontdiscoverycruises.com

The area's on-shore outdoor activities are also extensive,

so you may want to consider devoting a day to them in addition to your time on the water. Biking options revolve around the 12-mile **Island Line trail** while hiking possibilities include the nearby peaks of **Mt. Philo** and **Camel's Hump.** The former features a simple, hour-long hike that's perfect for families while the six-mile Monroe Trail up the latter leads past an eerie plane crash site to stunning 360-degree panoramic views from the top of Vermont's third highest and least developed peak.

Info: *Island Line trail*
Starts at Oakledge Park, 2 Flynn Ave
Mt. Philo State Park
Starts off Route 7, Charlotte
Tel. 802-425-2390
Camel's Hump
I-89 east to exit 11 to Route 2 and Camel's Hump Rd., Huntington.

The **Lake Champlain Islands** provide perhaps the most all-encompassing outdoor option of all. On the largest of the islands, **Grand Isle State Park** offers one of the area's prime campgrounds as well as great hiking, beaches and water sports. The island's just 15 minutes north of Burlington; to get there, take I-89 to exit 17 and travel west on Route 2 through South Hero.

Info: *Grand Isle State Park*
36 East Shore South, Grand Isle
Tel. 802-372-4300

Further up Route 2 just under an hour from Burlington, **North Hero State Park** is a more remote island gem not far from the Québec border. And if you really want to leave civilization (and your car) behind, consider tiny **Burton Island**. Accessible only by ferry, it makes a fine day trip with scenic views, secluded trails and canoeing spots. All told, there are more than 100 islands in Lake Champlain, and they offer enough variety to keep a serious outdoor enthusiast engaged for days.

Info: *Parks open May-Oct*
Burton Island Ferry departs

SIGHTS

Kamp Kill Kare State Park in St. Alban's Bay $2 each way.

For other attractions not far from Burlington, including such favorites as the Ben & Jerry's ice cream factory in Waterbury, see the Stowe area chapter.

OAKLEDGE PARK

Besides being an absolutely lovely place with a ton of outdoor amenities, Burlington's **Oakledge Park** has a couple of novel attractions too. The **large treehouse** at the south-

ern end of the park was the first such handicapped-accessible structure in the world, and the curious assemblage of stones at the end of Flynn Street is actually the **Burlington Earth Clock**, a 43-foot wide sundial that doubles as an art installation.

BEST SLEEPS & EATS

BURLINGTON

Lang House $$$

Once owned by a Green Mountain Boy, this Victorian home three blocks from Church Street offers both longstanding tradition and modern amenities. Recently renovated, the Lang's retained the high ceilings, vintage wood and plaster work of old as well as loads of period furniture. The lavish Captain Lyon room

boasts an antique, four-poster bed while the charming Van Ness room offers bay window views of Lake Champlain from the inn's turreted third floor. *Info: www.langhouse.com. 360 Main St. Tel. 877-919-9799. 11 rooms.*

SLEEPS & EATS

Willard Street Inn $$$

More castle than B&B, this turreted Victorian-style inn overlooks Lake Champlain from a hillside perch just a stone's throw from the University of Vermont campus. Its brick and white marble façade is adorned with ivy and a slate roof, and the wood-paneled, antique-laden interiors exude a similarly over the top, old-fashioned charm. Some rooms feature  lake and mountain views; request the Tower Room for the best vantages or the spacious Nantucket Room for additional space and luxury. Surrounded by gardens and historic homes, the inn's in a great neighborhood, though its one drawback is that it's a bit of a hike from downtown. *Info: www.willardstreetinn.com. 349 S. Willard St. Tel. 802-651-8710. 14 rooms.*

One of a Kind B&B $$-$$$

Decorated in rich earth and jewel tones, the two-room suite in this artist-run B&B exudes both class and whimsy, and the outdoors are a singular experience too. Lake Champlain is basically the backyard, and it's hard to say which is more inviting – breakfast on the front porch or the rope swing propelling you skyward from the garden to the lake. *Info: www.oneofakindbnb.com. 53 Lakeview Terrace. Tel. 802-862-5576. 2 rooms.*

Doubletree Hotel $$

Off I-89 and Route 2 halfway between downtown and the airport, the Doubletree is a reliable and convenient option for travelers on the go. Family-friendly and surprisingly charming – there's even a wood-paneled common room with fireplace – it provides the best hotel-style accommodations in the area and an abundance of extras such as a pool, workout room and complimentary shuttle service to and from Burlington International. *Info: www.doubletree.com. 1117 Williston Rd. Tel. 802-658-0250. 128 rooms.*

Sunset House B&B $$

This one-time boarding house turned bed and breakfast occupies a prime Main Street location midway between the waterfront and the Church Street marketplace. Rooms are merely basic, but the Queen Anne style house has plenty of character, and the area and reasonable rates rank the Sunset among the best of Burlington's mid-range options. *Info: www.sunsethousebb.com. 78 Main St. Tel. 802-864-3790. 4 rooms*

Hartwell House B&B $-$$

Burlington's best low-budget B&B is in a relaxed residential neighborhood just a short ride from town. The standard rooms share a bathroom and have hardwood floors, a skylight and either queen or twin beds. Pool access and a full breakfast are included, and the innkeepers are friendly and encouraging of pets. *Info: www.vermontbedandbreakfast.com. 170 Ferguson Ave. Tel. 802-658-9242. 3 rooms.*

Leunig's Bistro $$$

Church Street meets the Champs-Elysées at this old world bistro on the pedestrian mall. Amid chandeliers and a marble bar, an overhead sign urges you to "live well" – a task made all the easier by dishes such as roasted half duck and spaghetti squash Napoleon. The early bird special (before 5:45) is an outstanding value while the $100 tasting menu may be Burlington's best splurge. Leunig's also offers live music during the week and outdoor seating on the mall in summer. *Info: 115 Church St. Tel. 802-863-3759. Dinner daily, lunch Mon.-Fri., brunch Sat.-Sun. www.leunigsbistro.com.*

L'Amante $$$

It's easy to fall in love with L'Amante's regional Italian cuisine and casually elegant atmosphere one block from the waterfront. The wine list has won *Wine Spectator*'s award of excellence three years running while the menu melds Italian standards (gnocchi, risotto) and creative dishes like the must-sample squash blossom fritters and a mixed grill of Vermont quail, sausage and shrimp. *Info: 126 College St. Tel. 802-863-5200. Dinner Mon.-Sat. www.lamante.com.*

Taste $$-$$$

Taste pleases the senses with steak, seafood and vegetarian entrees in a supper club style atmosphere. The warm and inviting interior features exposed brick, copper and a 200-gallon aquarium, and cocktails and complimentary cheese and crackers are served at the maple and granite bar. Standout dishes include peanut-encrusted Atlantic salmon and a mock beef stew made with local seitan and Sam Smith porter. *Info: 112 Lake Street. Tel. 802-658-4844. Dinner daily. www.tasteofburlington.com.*

American Flatbread $$

Cross your favorite pizzeria with your favorite brewpub, and you'll have a pretty good idea of the artisanal pleasures awaiting you at American Flatbread. Aromas from the wood-fired oven mingle with the scents of yeast and hops, and there's no better pairing in Burlington than a custom flatbread pizza (made with local organic ingredients in creative combinations like pancetta with fire roasted zucchini) and a house-brewed Zero Gravity ale. Both the cozy dining room and bar area here fill quickly, so be prepared to wait for a table at peak times. *Info: 115 St. Paul St. Tel. 802-861-2999. Dinner daily, lunch Fri.-Sun. www.americanflatbread.com.*

Daily Planet $$

This funky yet classy bistro has been a staple of the Burlington dining scene for over 25 years. It offers both bar fare and traditional entrees such as rack of lamb and grilled New York strip steak in an inviting, well-lit space that also hosts monthly rotat-

ing art shows. *Info: 15 Center St. Tel. 802-862-9647. Dinner daily. www.dailyplanet15.com.*

A Single Pebble $$

Banquet-style seating and spicy Sichuan-style cooking character-ize this gourmet Chinese restaurant that was voted best of Vermont (by *Vermont Magazine*) just a few years back. The menu's delicacies include a succulent sesame catfish, top-notch noodle dishes and adventurous appetizers such as mock eel (actually mushroom) and spicy three river soup. *Info: 133-35 Bank St. Tel. 802-865-5200. Dinner daily, lunch Mon.-Sat. www.asinglepebble.com.*

Skinny Pancake $

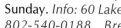

This lakeside creperie near the ECHO aquarium has a sunny patio and a long list of sweet and savory crepe varieties. It also makes a fine stop for cof-fee and a snack, or check out the popular folk and fondue music series Thursday through Sunday. *Info: 60 Lake St. Tel. 802-540-0188. Breakfast, lunch and dinner daily. www.skinnypancake.com.*

Big Fatty's BBQ $

A shades-wearing pig implores you to "put some south in your mouth" at this Memphis-style barbecue joint near the lake. A pig trough serves as a dining counter over which tender pulled pork, spare ribs, coleslaw and collards are passed. Portions are "Biblical", and the enormous sandwiches are splittable. *Info: 55 Main St. Tel. 802-864-5513. Lunch and dinner daily. www.maplestreetcatering.com.*

Bove's $

This family-owned Italian restaurant has been a Burlington

institution since 1941. Old-school in and out with a charming (if slightly decrepit) interior, Bove's is known around the region for its lasagna and pasta sauces (also jarred to go). Portions are large, and though the cuisine is less than innovative, it's hard to argue with a menu that spans mussels, meatballs and a $1.75 grilled cheese sandwich. *Info: 68 Pearl Street. Tel. 802-864-6651. Late lunch and dinner Tues.-Thurs., lunch and dinner Fri.-Sat. www.boves.com.*

Sneakers $

The line for the Burlington area's best weekend brunch often extends out the door of this unassuming storefront in downtown Winooski. Sneakers' Jump Start menu offers intriguing specials, though it's hard to top its cinnamon buns, novel varieties of eggs benedict and waffles topped with real maple syrup. *Info: 36 Main St., Winooski. Tel. 802-655-9081. Breakfast and lunch daily, brunch weekends. www.sneakersbistro.com.*

Stone Soup $

In addition to the hearty soups, this vegetarian-friendly favorite features sandwiches and a salad bar. Soups are served buffet-style along with fresh bread, and sandwich options range from turkey melts to vegan BLTs. *Info: 211 College St. Tel. 802-862-7616. Breakfast and lunch Mon.-Sat., dinner Tues.-Sat.*

Tiny Thai $

The best of Winooski's Asian restaurants serves cheap, well-spiced Thai fare just over the bridge from Burlington. Cheap multi-course lunches, pad Thai and the house's signature drunken noodles are all popular choices. *Info: 24 Main St., Winooski. Tel. 802-655-4888. Lunch and dinner Mon.-Sat.*

SHELBURNE

Inn at Shelburne Farms $$$

If you've ever had dreams of living a life of luxury on a 1,400-acre farm estate, the Inn at Shelburne Farms is there to answer them. The country retreat of 19th century Vermont luminaries Dr. William Seward and Lila Vanderbilt Webb, the hilltop Victorian home is set amid Frederick Law Olmsted-landscaped grounds

and looks out over the farm's vast meadows and gardens clear to Lake Champlain. Such outward charm is augmented by the inn's interior nooks and a genteel country décor built around vintage decorative patterns, pastels and wallpaper designs from the 1920s. Four cottages on the property hold additional guest rooms, and all come with welcome baskets and access to the farm's tours, trails and award-winning restaurant. Among the most expensive inns in Vermont, the Shelburne may also be the most outstanding. If you can afford it, you won't be disappointed. *Info: www.shelburnefarms.org. 1611 Harbor Rd. Tel. 802-985-8498. 28 rooms.*

Heart of the Village Inn $$$

On the National Register of Historic Places, this 1886 inn is a centerpiece of Shelburne Village. Its old-fashioned rooms are divided amongst the main inn and carriage house and are decorated with sleigh beds, original wood furnishings and other antiques. Other amenities include a wrap-around porch, reading loft and full breakfast. *Info: www.heartofthevillage.com. 5347 Shelburne Rd. Tel. 802-985-2800. 9 rooms.*

Café Shelburne $$$

Across a covered bridge from the Shelburne Museum, Café Shelburne offers the Burlington area's premier fine dining experience. Its traditional-contemporary French cuisine (escargot, coq au vin, filet mignon) has won the Vermont Grand award two years in a row, and the wine list and house-made chocolate truffles are equally fêted. *Info: 5573 Shelburne Rd. Tel. 802-985-3939. Dinner Tues.-Sat. www.cafeshelburne.com.*

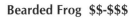

Bearded Frog $$-$$$

Chef Michel Mahe's latest venture (he also owns Bristol's Bobcat Café and the Black Sheep in Vergennes) is this classic gastropub in the Shelburne Inn. Tucked alongside an independent book shop and toy store, it offers both patio and fireside seating, grilled flatbread specials and gourmet variations on comfort food such as venison and chorizo meatloaf. *Info: 5247 Shelburne Rd., Shelburne. Tel. 802-985-9877. Dinner daily. www.thebeardedfrog.com.*

ESSEX & JERICHO

Inn at Essex $$$

Known for its culinary attractions, the Inn at Essex offers fine

dining and large-scale resort accommodations in an outlet town seven miles outside Burlington. The AAA Four Diamond property features a brand-new spa, tennis courts and a heated pool, and the recently rede-signed guest rooms (28 of which are suites) are decorated in warm pastels that lend a country-contemporary feel. The inn's main attraction, however, are its three restaurants run under the auspices of the New England Culinary Institute. Butler's (*see review below*) offers some of the best high end dining in the region as well as cooking classes, demonstrations and custom dining parties for groups. *Info: www.vtculinaryresort.com. 70 Essex Way, Essex Junction. Tel. 802-878-1100. 120 rooms.*

Butler's Restaurant $$$

The most formal of the three restaurants at the Inn at Essex is helmed by New England Culinary Institute students eager to show their gourmet chops. The atmosphere is refined, and the classic menu spotlights steaks, scallops, lamb chops and a stellar spread of Vermont cheeses. A range of options from *prix fixe* to buffet brunch are available. For a more relaxed atmosphere at this culinary resort of sorts, try the casual American fare served

SLEEPS & EATS

in the **Tavern.** *Info: 70 Essex Way, Essex. Tel. 802-878-1100. Dinner daily, Sunday brunch. www.vtculinaryresort.com.*

Joe's Snack Bar $
Joe's has been serving burgers, hand-cut fries and "creemees" at a bend in the road outside Jericho since 1950. Order at the window of this old-school snack bar, then indulge at the picnic tables out back. *Info: 45 Route 15, Jericho. Tel. 802-899-3934. Lunch and dinner daily. Closed in winter.*

THE ISLANDS
North Hero House $$-$$$
This historic 1891 inn has a simply amazing setting. Two levels of front porches and a glassed-in dining area look out onto Lake Champlain, as do many of the guest rooms. Rooms are distributed amongst four buildings, including the main inn. Request one with a lake view that's also away from the road (the house is right on Route 2), and be sure to take advantage of the swimming, kayaking and other lakeside activities that are Hero's hallmarks. *Info: www.northherohouse.com. Route 2, North Hero. Tel. 888-525-3644. 26 rooms. Open May-Nov.*

Apple Island Resort $
This 188-acre all-purpose resort on South Hero Island features a spa, a marina and even a nine-hole golf course. Lodging is cheap and abundant and ranges from one-room cabins to a full service campground. *Info: www.appleislandresort.com. 71 Route 2, South Hero. Tel. 802-372-3800.*

BEST SHOPPING

Burlington Area

The **Church Street marketplace** is Burlington's commercial heart. The pretty, tree-lined pedestrian mall is lined with small and national retailers, and pushcart vendors and performance artists add options and ambiance. The Saturday Farmers' Market makes the already vibrant street even livelier and is a great place to pick up local crafts. *Info*: www.churchstreetmarketplace.com.

Beyond the marketplace, Burlington offers shopping for every taste, whether you're seeking vintage fashions from the **Old Gold** consignment shop (*180 Main St.*) or sporting goods from the **Outdoor Gear Exchange** (*152 Cherry St.*).

For outlets, the **Essex Shoppes** (*21 Essex Way, Essex, Tel. 802-878-2851*) are just a 15-minute drive from Burlington via I-89, Route 15 and Route 289 East. More intimate shopping side trips can be had in Burlington's sister city of Winooski and in the village of Shelburne. Just south of Burlington via Route 7, **Shelburne** is home to a small historic district of shops, but its most famous store is the **Vermont Teddy Bear Factory shop** (*6655 Shelburne Rd., Tel. 802-985-3001*) that's just a mile outside town (*see photo below*). For more info on Burlington area shopping, visit *www.vermont.org*.

BEST NIGHTLIFE & ENTERTAINMENT

Burlington

As both a college town and Vermont's biggest city, Burlington offers an extremely vibrant late-night scene. **Nectar's** (*188 Main St., Tel. 802-658-4771*), where the jam band Phish got its start, is a prime venue for live music, and **Higher Ground**, in South Burlington (*1214 Williston Rd., Tel. 802-652-0777*), books national acts as well. The **Flynn Center for the Performing Arts** (*153 Main St., Tel. 802-863-5966*) – once a vaudeville house – now hosts Broadway theater, dance, world music and more in its restored art deco headquarters downtown. For an up-to-date barometer of arts goings-on, pick up the free *Seven Days* newspaper that's available around town or check it out online at *www.7nvt.com*.

Church Street is home to a number of bar-bistros and dimly romantic cocktail lounges such as the **One-Half Lounge** (*136 1/2 Church St., Tel. 802-865-0012*). **American Flatbread** (*115 St. Paul Street, Tel. 802-861-2999*) and the **Vermont Brewing Company** (*144 College Street, Tel. 802-865-0500*) serve some of the better house beers in town. The former is brick-oven warm and classy while the latter is larger and popular with college students. In the hole-in-the-wall category, the cozy **Three Needs** brewpub on College Street (*Tel. 802-658-0889*) serves its own beer alongside a secret "Duff" special. Burlington has a great café culture too, from the bohemian **Radio Bean** coffeeshop (*8 N. Winooski Ave., Tel. 802-660-9346*), which hosts live music most nights, to the more refined **Dobrá Tea Room** on Church Street (*Tel. 802-951-2424*).

BEST SPORTS & RECREATION

Burlington

Burlington's the place to be if you want to see a semi-major sporting event in the state. The **University of Vermont athletic department** (*Tel. 802-656-4410, www.uvm.edu*) fields competitive men's and women's squads in a number of NCAA sports, including basketball and hockey. Baseball fans will want to catch the Washington Nationals-affiliated **Vermont Lake Monsters** in the friendly confines of **Centennial Field** (*East Ave., Tel. 802-655-4200*). It's not the major leagues, but then neither are the prices (no tickets more than $8). On a summer night, there's no better sports-related family experience in Vermont.

Burlington's outdoor recreation opportunities revolve around Lake Champlain. Set sail with a boat rental from the **Community Sailing Center** (*1 Lake St., Tel. 802-864-2499*) or jump right in with a scuba lesson from the **Waterfront Diving Center** (*214 Battery St., Tel. 800-283-7282*). You can also rent a kayak at North Beach, or simply kick back and relax at Burlington's largest and most popular beach, which can be found just off the Burlington Bike Path at the end of Institute Road off North Avenue. **Oak Ledge Park**, on the south side of town at the end of Flynn Avenue (*see sidebar on page 180*), is another popular lakeside spot for swimming, sunning and summertime relaxation.

The 7.6-mile **Burlington Bike Path** starts at Oak Ledge Park, then follows the shoreline through the Waterfront Park and up to the northern end of the Winooski River, where it merges with the Colchester bike path to form the 12-mile Island Line trail. The non-profit cycling group **Local Motion** (*1 Steele St., Tel. 802-652-2453*) has a base near the Waterfront Park and will rent you a bike and point you in the right direction. For more information on outdoor recreation in, on and around Lake Champlain, visit *www.enjoyburlington.com*.

SPORTS & RECREATION

For recreation options outside of Burlington, you can either head inland to the neighboring mountains or off shore to the lake islands. Fifteen miles north of Burlington via I-89 and Route 2, **Grand Isle State Park** (*Tel. 802-372-4300*) is the best island destination. It offers great hiking, beaches and water sports as well as one of the area's top campgrounds. Inland hiking options include **Mount Philo State Park** in Charlotte (*Tel. 802-425-2390*). Off Route 7, it offers a variety of mid-range hikes that culminate in views of the Adirondack Mountains and Lake Champlain. More challenging terrain can be found at **Camel's Hump**, the third largest (and least developed) of Vermont's peaks. Close to I-89, it has a variety of popular trails, the best of which is the six-mile **Monroe Trail** that takes you above the tree line to dramatic 360-degree views of the surrounding mountains.

9. THE NORTHEAST KINGDOM

HIGHLIGHTS
▲ St. Johnsbury

▲ Cabot Cheese Factory

▲ Crafstbury Common, Newport

▲ Jay Peak/Burke Mountain

▲ Lake Willoughby, Lake Memphremagog

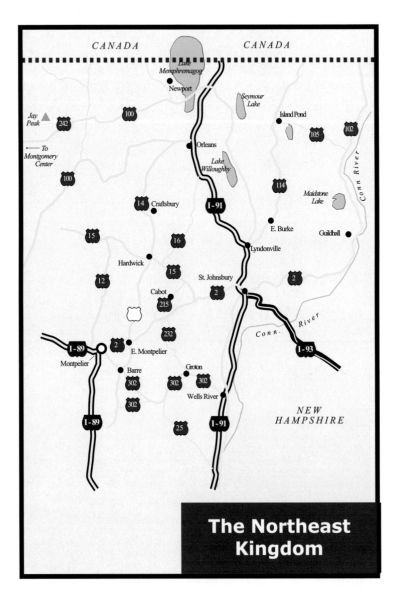

The Northeast Kingdom

INTRO

Vermont's Northeast Kingdom is the wildest, most rural part of the state. Relatively remote and less touristed, it contains some of Vermont's **most striking landscapes** as well as a number of attractive small

COORDINATES

St. Johnsbury lies at the intersection of I-93 and I-91. **Craftsbury** is on Rt. 14, **Cabot Cheese** on Rt. 215, **Hardwick** at Rt's 14 and 15, **Lake Willoughby** on Rt. 5A, **Burke Mountain** on Rt. 114, **Newport** off I-91 and **Jay Peak** on Rt. 242.

towns connected by classic country roads. Domain to royal blue lakes, majestic mountains and more forest than any other region, the Kingdom bursts with a fairy tale beauty true to its name.

ST. JOHNSBURY SIGHTS IN A DAY

Tucked in the Kingdom's southeast corner at the intersection of Routes 91 and 93, **St. Johnsbury** is the region's largest and most accessible town. While away most of your day exploring its boutiques and cultural attractions, including the Fairbanks Museum and the Athenaeum, then make the short drive down scenic Route 2 to the Cabot Creamery.

Among Vermont's most authentic small town experiences, St. Johnsbury offers an unusual blend of ruggedness and Victorian charm. All of ten blocks, it nonetheless has two distinct areas. **Railroad Street** is the town's commercial core, with an appealing range of shops from outdoor

outfitters to specialty food purveyors. Steep Eastern Avenue connects this consumer district with residential Main Street. **Grand Victorian homes** line this broad, graceful boulevard and get more lavish as you progress northward. As you make your way, you'll pass the prestigious St. Johnsbury Academy prep school and historic houses of worship like the South Congregational Church with its conical spire and open bell tower.

Main Street's cornerstone, the **Fairbanks Museum**, stands at the top of the hill. Built in the late 19th century by a local industrialist, its striking stone quarters contain the area's best natural history museum

SIGHTS

SIGHTS

and the state's only public planetarium. The 175,000-object collection includes artifacts like fossils, tools and toys; curiosities like John Hampson's bug mosaics; and an array of preserved animals. Planetarium shows shine on weekend afternoons, though the Eye on the Sky weather gallery illuminates the heavens daily and provides a fascinating look at the forces that shape global climates.

Info: 1302 Main St
Open Mon.-Sat., 9am-5pm, Sun. 1-5pm. Closed Mon. in winter. Planetarium shows Sat.-Sun. 1:30 pm
Admission $6
Tel. 802-748-2372
www.fairbanksmuseum.org

Main Street's other aesthetic anchor is the **St. Johnsbury Athenaeum**. The country's oldest art gallery (in original form) doubles as a public library and is thus as full of finely bound books as classic American paintings. The Poole antiquarian book collection and the giant Albert Bierstadt canvas opposite the gallery entrance are among the Athenaeum's highlights, though it's a must-visit as much for the building itself – a National Historic Landmark – as the objects within. Built in the French Second Empire style, the sturdy red brick building dates to 1871, and its interiors are rich with elaborate woodwork, elongated windows, spiral stairways and a gilded sense of days gone by.

Info: 1171 Main St
Open Mon.-Wed. 10am-8pm, Tues., Thurs.-Fri. 10am-5:30pm, Sat. 9:30am-4pm
Admission free
Tel. 802-748-8291
www.stjathenaeum.org

I DUB THEE NORTHEAST KINGDOM

Senator George Aiken is credited with giving the Kingdom its royal moniker. During a 1949 speech in Lyndonville he declared, "This is such beautiful country up here. It ought to be called the Northeast Kingdom of Vermont," and the title's stuck ever since.

SIGHTS

St. Johnsbury's historic attractions are steeped with local color, but for even more distinctive Vermont flavor, you'll have to hop in the car and drive to Cabot, home of the **Cabot Cheese** cooperative. Thirty minutes from St. Johnsbury via Route 2 west and Route 215, the original Cabot Village factory has been churning out its famous cheddar here since 1919. Friendly locals lead tours of the premises and explain how cheese gets from cow to cracker as curd-milling machines and white-hatted workers imperviously prepare the product for market. As informative as the tour can be, the best part of the Cabot experience is undeniably the gift shop's sample table, where you can spear cubes of every cheddar imaginable, from extra sharp to chili lime.

Info: 2878 Main St., Cabot Open daily 9am-5pm June-Oct.; Mon.-Sat. 9am-4pm Nov.-May; Mon.-Sat. 10am-4pm Jan Tours $2 Call ahead to confirm cheesemaking Tel. 800-837-4261 www.cabotcheese.com

A late afternoon Cabot tour and leisurely return drive will have you back to St. Johnsbury in time for an early evening stroll and dinner at **Elements**, St. Johnsbury's best bistro (see Best Sleeps & Eats).

A WEEKEND IN THE ST. JOHNSBURY AREA

For a wonderful weekend in the Kingdom, **use St. Johnsbury as a base** for getting out into the country. Take in cultural attractions like the Fairbanks Museum, then hit the road for a memorable loop through enchanting small towns and the Kingdom's spectacular **Lake Region**.

SIGHTS

National Geographic recently named St. Johnsbury its **#1 small town for adventure**, and the designation fits – partially on personality and partially for its easy access to the more untrammeled parts of the Kingdom. The one-day plan above provides considerable exposure to the former. Spread its suggestions over Friday night and the better part of Saturday, with an eye towards skipping town by mid-afternoon.

As in the one-day plan, make the **Cabot Cheese Factory** off Route 215 your first stop outside St. Johnsbury. Take a late afternoon tour, toothpick enough cheese samples to tide you over to dinner, and then make the 10-mile drive up South Walden Road and Route 15 to Hardwick.

Once a hardscrabble hub of the area's granite industry, **Hardwick** today is part agricultural center, part quaint small town. Set on the Lamoille River, it's at the forefront of Vermont's burgeoning Community Supported Agriculture movement that directly links farmers with consumers and local restaurants.

Some of the best evidence of the movement's success – and Hardwick's renaissance – is the food at **Claire's**. Ultrawelcoming with light hardwood floors and a cozy bar in back, Claire's is the kind of restaurant you wish your hometown had – creatively classy, affordable and dedicated to the local community (*see Best Sleeps & Eats*).

After dinner, you can either hunker down in Hardwick for the night – the Kimball House bed and breakfast being your best lodging option – or drive on into the town of **Craftsbury**, where you'll find a number of attractive inns and bed and breakfasts. Ten miles north of Hardwick via Route 14, it's one of Vermont's most picturesque villages and the starting point for a spectacular Sunday in the Kingdom.

Surrounded by rolling green hills and dairy farms, historic **Craftsbury Common** is Woodstock's less gentrified northern cousin. It has all the **classic village** hallmarks, from town green to antiques scene, with a fraction of the tourists. The Craftsbury charter dates to 1781 and apparently included language requiring every house to be made of white clapboard. Okay, that's not quite true, but it took some kind of foresight for a town to retain such architectural charm, from colonial and Federal style buildings down to a prototypical general store. Old movie buffs may recognize the town as the backdrop for Alfred Hitchcock's classic comedy *The Trouble with Harry* (1955).

Take a Sunday morning tour of the town, focusing on the village green area and diverging into the centuries-old cemetery on the south side of town. If you're feeling athletic, the **Craftsbury Outdoor Center** offers a range of recreation options. Located on a high plateau, its 80 miles of beautiful trails make for excellent biking in warmer weather and cross country skiing in winter.

Info: 535 Lost Nation Rd
Tel. 802-586-7767
www.craftsbury.com

For an even more remarkable outdoor experience, follow Route 14 north along the Black River to Route 58 to Route 5A and **Lake Willoughby**. This is a beautiful drive through completely undeveloped country, but it's nothing compared to what awaits at your destination: the most gorgeous lake in perhaps all of New England.

In a region filled with natural beauty, **Lake Willoughby** is the Kingdom's crystal heart, an impossibly beautiful oasis teardropped into a stunning mountain landscape. The

SIGHTS

cliffs of **Mount Pisgah** (*see photo above*) and Mount Hor rise up from the lake's surface, and you can enjoy their beauty any number of ways, starting with staring out the window slack-jawed as you drive around it along Route 5A. Whether you circle its shimmering surface by car or canoe, kick back on its beaches or hike the surrounding trails, Willoughby is an absolute must as the culmination of your weekend. For more details on the outdoor recreation options in the area, including the steeply spectacular Pisgah Trail, see the one-week plan below.

ALTERNATIVE PLAN

With its pristine alpine setting and moderate size, Burke Mountain feels like the middle of nowhere, but at just 20 miles outside St. Johnsbury, it's the Kingdom's most accessible spot for serious outdoor recreation. The mountain receives nearly 250 inches of snow annually, so good powder is rarely a problem, and Kingdom Trails – Vermont's largest recreational trail network – is among the world's top mountain biking destinations. Whether you're riding, biking or snowshoeing, pick up a trail guide at East Burke Sports and explore the area's barn-fronted fields and backwoods roads to your heart's content. *Info: 439 Rte. 114. Tel. 802-626-3215. Buy required $10 trail pass here or at the welcome center behind the Burke General Store.*

A WEEK IN THE NORTHEAST KINGDOM

A week in the Northeast Kingdom is pure magic. Sure, there are regions with more prominent towns and tourist attractions, but nowhere in Vermont will you so strongly connect with the natural world. Think wide-open, light-streaked skies, mountains as far as the eye can see, lakes as clear as they are deep. It's often assumed that you have to head out west or into Canada for these sorts of landscapes, so it may be a revelation to find such big country in little old Vermont. But trust me, it's out there – and with a week in the Kingdom, it's yours to discover.

The lower part of the Kingdom is still the place to start your northeast adventure. The stalwart towns of the southeast Kingdom – **St. Johnsbury**, **Craftsbury** and **Cabot** – merit a good three days if you follow the weekend plan for the area and add in another handful of local highlights.

Of particular note are a pair of attractions on St. Johnsbury's outer edge. Only a mile outside town is the **Maple Grove Farms Maple Museum and Factory**. The country's largest packer of pure maple syrup's been in business for nearly a century, and you can see how they make their signature maple candies with a

tour of the factory and adjoining Sugar House Museum.

Info: 1052 Portland St
Shop open Mon.-Fri. 8am-5pm May-Dec. Tours run 8am-2pm
Admission $1
Tel. 802-748-5141
www.maplegrove.com

Just a couple of minutes further along Route 2, Stephen Huneck's **Dog Chapel** pays tribute to man's best friend with distinctive, dog-oriented art. Sculptures and a small, lab-weathervaned church with stained glass windows celebrate the human canine bond, and the trails criss-crossing the artist's 400-acre hilltop farm are perfect for a stroll, particularly if you're traveling with a four-legged friend.

Info: 143 Parks Rd
Tel. 800-449-2580
Open Mon.-Sat. 10am-5pm, Sun. 11am-4pm
www.dogmt.com

If you're looking for more outdoor options, the **Groton State Forest** has 25,000 + acres brimming with lakes, trails and wildlife. Between St. Johnsbury and Montpelier on the Kingdom's southern edge, it's the second largest protected area in Vermont and a paradise for hiking, biking, horseback riding and swimming. Groton Forest Highway/ Route 232 runs north/south through the forest and provides access to all six of its state parks.

Outside St. Johnsbury the Kingdom is speckled with small towns that lend themselves to extended appreciation or a quick drive through. Among the prettiest in the southeast part is **Peacham**. Its porched-in country store, maple-shadowed cemetery and views of the White Mountains make it perhaps the purest of all Vermont's colonial-era villages.

Outside of this sort of simple beauty, such towns aren't all that notable on their own, but nowhere is the old adage of

"pleasure in the journey" as true. Passing through these towns is like passing through time, and the countryside in between is like something out of a calendar, that single old house at the crest of a hill, the falling down barn set between forest and pasture, the impassively grazing cows. They're all painted with the same nostalgic brush, and it feels like a privilege to share their space, whether for a week or a day or an instant.

FALL FOLIAGE FESTIVALS

There are seven Kingdom towns that host foliage festivals in late September and early October: Barnet; Cabot; Groton; Peacham; Plainfield; St. Johnsbury; and Walden. *Info*: www.nekchamber.com.

The further north you go, the more vivid the landscape gets. Roughly midway between St. Johnsbury and Canada along

🏃 Route 5A, the gem of the Lake Region – **Lake Willoughby** – will take your breath away all over again. Like something out of Glacier Park or the extreme northwest, it's a huge and idyllic place, all cliffs, clouds and shimmering surface, with unparalleled outdoor opportunities to match. Public beaches on the north and south ends of the lake let you bask in its beauty while a variety of trail and adventure-oriented activities await the more intrepid. Hike the precipitous **Pisgah Trail** (three hours top to bottom) or the moderate **Herbert Hawkes Trail** (a half-day trek up Mt. Hor) for spectacular views and terrain. If you really want to live on the edge, sign up for a rock or ice climbing expedition through **Vermont Adventure Tours**. The Pisgah trail head is half a mile south of lake; look for small parking area along Route 5A. For the Hawkes trail head, drive through the Pisgah parking area and continue 1.7 miles to parking area on left.

Info: Vermont Adventure Tours
Tel. 802-773-3343
www.vermontadventuretours.com

This area is so beautiful, and the outdoor activities so varied, that settling in for a couple days is highly recommended. On the shores of the lake along Route 5A in Westmore, the **WilloughVale Inn** offers tranquilly luxurious accommodations in lakeside cottages that are as ideal for romance as for a family oriented outdoor escape (*see Best Sleeps & Eats*).

Establishing a base here allows you to explore the Kingdom's famous **Lake Region** more in depth. Extending up from Willoughby further into the northeast, this range of picture perfect pools includes **Seymour Lake** (near the town of Morgan) and **Echo Lake** (just south of Seymour Lake near East Charleston). Both are prime destinations for canoeing, kayaking, swimming and fishing.

Brownington is your best in-town option around these parts. It's a charming assemblage of farmland and historic homes, chief among them being the **Old Stone House Museum**. Once the homestead of Alexander Twilight, the country's first African American state legislator, it today houses the local his-

SIGHTS

torical society's collection and exhibits focusing on 19th century life in the area.

Info: 109 Old Stone House Rd., Brownington
Open Wed.-Sun. 11am-5pm, mid May-mid Oct
Admission $5
Tel. 802-754-2022
www.oldstonehousemuseum.org

With your remaining time, head deeper still into the Kingdom via **Route 91**. The region's main artery runs all the way from St. Johnsbury to Newport (a 45 mile trip) and on through to Canada. This is some kind of drive, taking you through forest and farmland, past covered bridges and country stores and even near a couple towns of note: Barton, home to the Sugar Mill maple farm and the best base for exploring **Crystal Lake State Park**; and Glover, world renowned as the residence of **Bread and Puppet Theater**.

Info: 753 Heights Rd., Glover
Open daily 10am-5pm May-Oct
Admission free
Tel. 802-525-1271
www.breadandpuppet.org

Newport is the north country's most noteworthy town and the best spot from which to explore its outer bounds. Newport might have a reputation as one of America's best small towns if it wasn't so cold. Indian summer elsewhere in Vermont pretty much means winter up here along the Canadian border. It's said cold builds character, and Newport, with a sharp little downtown and serene lakefront setting, isn't lacking for that. Eat a sweet little lunch on Main Street at Newport Natural Foods and Bakery, then spend an afternoon (weather permitting) out on **Lake Memphremagog**. The 40-mile long lake (most of which is in Canada) has a boardwalk, a pier and a beach along its southern edge and is home (some say) to a giant lake monster named Gog.

Info: Newport Natural Foods
66 Main St
Tel. 802-334-2626
www.newportnaturalfoods.com

Newport also serves as the gateway to the **Jay Peak** resort area. Twenty minutes from town and just south of the Canadian border, it's Vermont's **northernmost ski**

🏃 **destination** (*see photo below*) and often has serious snow at times when other resorts are an icy mess. Dedicated skiers will want to spend a couple days here navigating challenging glades like Valhalla and the (comparatively) peaceful Beaver Pond. With its extreme cold and wind and emphasis on intermediate and expert terrain, Jay is not always for the faint of heart, but it rewards hardy beginners and serious skiers with an outsized outdoor experience. The resort also offers a range of other activities, from mountainside tram rides (ideal for leaf peeping) to hiking trails to New England's newest championship golf course.

Info: 4850 Route 242, Jay Tel. 802-988-2611 www.jaypeakresort.com

However you conclude your week in the Kingdom, leave yourself time for a leisurely ride out. If you're heading back to Burlington and points west, stop to enjoy the **incredible scenery along Route 100**. Or if you're driving back towards Boston and the southeast, you can get one last eyeful by taking the circuitous way along Routes 105 and 114 back to I-91. For these and most other extended drives through the Kingdom, keep a careful eye on your fuel gauge – gas stations can be few and far between in this part of the state, and just because a town's on the map doesn't mean you can fill up there. For more suggestions in the vicinity of the Northeast Kingdom, see the Stowe area chapter.

SIGHTS

BEST SLEEPS & EATS

ST. JOHNSBURY
Rabbit Hill Inn $$$

This AAA Four Diamond property nine miles southeast of St. Johnsbury on Route 18 is among the Kingdom's most romantic

inns. Built in 1795, it burnishes its history with a lavish country style that's equal parts antiques, fireplaces and exposed beams and luxury amenities such as double whirlpool tubs and an award-winning on-premises restaurant. Add this to the inn's 15 acres of countryside, and it's easy to see why Rabbit Hill routinely makes the shortlist of New England's best places to propose. *Info: www.rabbithillinn.com. 48 Lower Waterford Rd, Lower Waterford. Tel. 802-748-5168. 19 rooms.*

Estabrook House $$

With its porch, turret and stained glass features, this stately Victorian structure exudes character. Just a quarter mile off I-91, Estabrook House is a strong value for its location, bay window views and breakfast buffet. The only possible drawback is that one bath is shared among the rooms. *Info: www.estabrookhouse.com. 1596 Main St. Tel. 802-751-8261. 4 rooms.*

Fairbanks Inn $-$$

Offering standard hotel amenities at motel prices, the Fairbanks Inn provides the best of both. Rooms are spacious and well maintained, and some have balconies. The outdoor heated pool and the nicely manicured grounds are a notch above expectations as well. *Info: www.stjay.com. 401 Western Ave. Tel. 866-359-8204. 45 rooms.*

Seyon Lodge $

This lodge on Noyes Pond in Groton State Forest provides private and semi private rooms on state parkland about 30 miles southwest of St. Johnsbury. Cheap and cozy with a fireplaced common area and all-inclusive meals, it's an incredible value from which to explore the lower reaches of the Kingdom. The pristine setting provides access to hiking, swimming, fly fishing and other outdoor activities. *Info: www.vtstateparks/htm/seyon.cfm. 2967 Seyon Pond Rd., Groton. Tel. 802-584-3829. 8 rooms.*

Rabbit Hill Inn $$$

Rabbit Hill's candlelit cuisine is as elegantly country as the inn itself. Three-course meals start with from-scratch soups and Francophile appetizers (frogs legs, foie gras), then move on to hearty deluxe entrees such as rabbit and short ribs. It all adds up to St. Johnsbury's most lavish gourmet experience. Reservations are required. *Info: 48 Lower Waterford Rd., Lower Waterford. Tel. 802-748-5168. Dinner daily. www.rabbithillinn.com.*

Elements $$-$$$

You'll want a more than a periodic table at Elements once you partake of its charming atmosphere and creative local cuisine. The location in a converted mill overlooking the Passumpsic River belies a cutting edge menu and wine list that would stand up well on any urban culinary scene. Signature dishes such as the Elemental salad and smoked trout and apple cakes make Elements St. Johnsbury's best dining experience and put it at the vanguard of a new wave of Vermont restaurants synthesizing country cooking and the urban bistro experience. *Info: 98 Mill St. Tel. 802-748-8400. Dinner Tues.-Sat. Reservations recommended. www.elementsfood.com.*

Kham's Thai Cuisine $$

Serving real deal Thai dishes in an unlikely location, Kham's is known for its authentic noodle soups, reasonable prices and friendly service. If you're craving Asian cuisine, this is the best option in the Kingdom. *Info: 1112 Memorial Dr. Tel. 802-751-8424. Lunch and dinner Wed.-Mon.*

Dylan's Café $-$$

Bright, colorful and cosmopolitan, Dylan's is known for its extensive menu of sandwiches served on locally baked breads. It's pricey by small town standards but is hands down the town's most delicious and refined midday option. *Info: 378 Railroad St. Tel. 802-748-6748. Breakfast and lunch daily.*

Anthony's Diner $

Classic diner fare, including house-made chips and a variety of burgers, are served daily here, though Anthony's also uses its share of locally grown organic produce. Evening hours are limited but often feature all-you-can-eat specials. *Info: 50 Railroad St. Tel. 802-748-3613. Breakfast, lunch and dinner daily.*

HARDWICK
Kimball House $$

This charming yellow and green, porch-framed Victorian is

Hardwick's best B&B option. It features gardens, a homey dining room and a trio of upstairs guest rooms that are clean, comfortable and share two baths between them. *Info: www.kimballhouse.com. 173 Glenside Ave. Tel. 802-472-6228. 3 rooms.*

Claire's Restaurant $$

If you have but one meal in the Kingdom, have it at Claire's. The cooperatively-owned restaurant's slogan of "local ingredients open to the world" is realized in creative yet down-home dishes like fork-tender brisket molé and pot pies crammed with locally grown root vegetables. Visually pleasing with light hardwood floors and framed local art, Claire's also boasts a cozy back bar with local beer and wine and live music on Thursdays. It all adds up to a dining experience that's remarkably simple, delicious and all too rare. *Info: 41 S. Main St. Tel. 802-472-7053. Dinner Thurs.-Tues., Sun. brunch. www.clairesvt.com.*

CRAFTSBURY
Inn on the Common $$$

Fronted by trees and a classic white fence, this quintessential Kingdom property offers luxury accommodations in three restored Federal style houses. Hand-stitched quilts and four-poster beds distinguish the guest rooms, some of which feature fireplaces or woodburning stoves. Televisions are refreshingly absent, and you won't miss technology one bit once you wander the grounds, kick back in the inn's cozy library/bar or dine at the on-premises Trellis restaurant. Pets are welcome in the Chandler House. *Info: www.innonthecommon.com. 1162 N. Craftsbury Rd. Tel. 802-586-9619. 17 rooms.*

Highland Lodge $$$

Just a short drive southeast from Craftsbury, this family-owned inn and Nordic center is set on an expansive property overlooking Caspian Lake. With 50 kilometers of groomed trails in winter and private tennis courts and a sandy lakeside beach in summer, the Highland is an ideal outdoor destination. Its inn rooms and hillside cottages are also a draw for their farmhouse décor and sweeping views of the lake. Upstairs rooms offer the best vantages. Common areas are cozy and offer everything from a Steinway piano to a foosball table. *Info: www.highlandlodge.com. 1608 Craftsbury Rd., Greensboro. Tel. 802-533-2647. 18 rooms.*

Craftsbury Outdoor Center $$

A top destination for Nordic skiing and sculling, the Outdoor Center provides comfortable, no-frills lodging following a long day on the trails or the water. The wide variety of accommodations ranges from private lakeside cottages to apartment-style lodging with private and shared baths. Rates include a trails pass, three all-you-can-eat meals and access to the center's sauna and weight room. *Info: www.craftsbury.com. 535 Lost Nation Rd. Tel. 802-586-7767. 47 rooms.*

Highland Lodge Restaurant $$$

Whether you enjoy a four-course dinner on the porch or in the candlelit dining room, the Highland Lodge offers great ambiance. Homemade breads are a treat, the dinner menu changes daily and lighter fare is also available. *Info: 1608 Craftsbury Rd., Greensboro. Tel. 802-533-2647. www.highlandlodge.com. Breakfast, lunch and dinner daily.*

Trellis at Inn on the Common $$$

Inn on the Common guests can enjoy Craftsbury's classiest dining room throughout the week while non-guests can reserve a table on weekends. The innkeeper doubles as the chef, and his four-course meals are built around traditional New England ingredients. The candlelit dining room is among Vermont's most romantic. *Info: 1162 N. Craftsbury Rd. Tel. 802-586-9619. Dinner Fri.-Sat., dinner daily for inn guests. www.innonthecommon.com.*

LAKE WILLOUGHBY
WilloughVale Inn $$$

Enjoy tranquil and luxurious lakeside lodging at one of the most beautiful spots in all of Vermont. Choose from among the main

inn's 10 rooms, including the standout Governor Aiken Room with private porch and fireside Jacuzzi tub, or opt for one of the romantic cottages spread across the property. New, expansive hillside cottages offer stunning views of Willoughby Gap while the quartet of luxury cabins right on the lake have kitchens, fireplaces, decks and dock access. *Info: www.willoughvale.com. Route 5A South, Westmore. Tel. 802-525-4123. 18 rooms.*

Angie's Haven $$

This 1894 farmhouse on 82 acres provides homey, affordable accommodations just a few miles northwest of Lake Willoughby. The pair of light-filled guest rooms are decorated with quilts and antique furniture, and the second floor suite has a king size bed and a king size view of Willoughby Gap. Pets are permitted, and breakfast is included. *Info: www.angies-havenbb.com. 2587 Schoolhouse Rd., Brownington. Tel. 802-754-6182. 3 rooms.*

Rodgers Country Inn $
In the family since the 1800s, the Rodgers property is home to a farmhouse-style inn with basic rooms (rentable by the night or by the week) as well as a beautiful secluded cabin for added space and privacy. From the location (near Bread and Puppet Theater and within a half hour's drive of three different lakes) to the home cooked meals (breakfast and dinner) offered family-style in the dining room, the Rodgers offers great value and a real Vermont experience. *Info: www.virtualvermont.com/rodgers. 582 Rodgers Rd., West Glover. Tel. 802-525-6677. 5 rooms.*

WilloughVale Inn $$-$$$
The views of Lake Willoughby and the surrounding mountains are the chief draw of the WilloughVale's casual dining room. For a drink and more informal fare, try the Tap Room Bar. Both are closed in winter. *Info: Route 5A South, Westmore. Tel. 802-525-4123. Dinner Wed.-Sun. www.willoughvale.com.*

Candlepin Restaurant $$
This family restaurant is adjacent to a bowling alley a half-mile north of the village center. It's popular for a menu of homestyle favorites that includes steak, sandwiches and an extensive salad bar. *Info: 558 Barton-Orleans Rd., Barton. Tel. 802-525-6513. Breakfast, lunch and dinner daily.*

BURKE
Burke Slopeside Lodging $$$
For townhouse-style vacation rentals near the base lodge, this is the place. Options range from private homes to multi-level condos such as Burkeside that are just steps from the lifts. *Info: Tel. 802-626-3066. www.burkeslopesidelodging.com*

Inn at Mountain View Farm $$$
For a true rural retreat, escape to this classic 440-acre farm along one of the Kingdom's most beautiful country roads. Replete with red barns, trails and an animal sanctuary, the property is as

sprawling as it is stunning, and the 13 guest rooms (divided between the farmhouse and a former creamery) are luxurious without being pretentious. Furnishings include ebony and four-poster beds, handmade quilts and leather reading chairs. A classic country breakfast, afternoon tea and access to Kingdom Trails are all included. *Info: www.innmtnview.com. 3383 Darling Hill Rd., East Burke. Tel. 802-626-9924. 14 rooms.*

Wildflower Inn $$-$$$

The Wildflower's village-like setting includes cottages, three-room suites and simple inn-style accommodations. All are enriched by views of the surrounding 570 acres, which offer all sorts of outdoor

opportunities, from horse-drawn wagon rides to skating and sledding. The inn's petting barn and dog friendly policies also make it a favorite of animal lovers. *Info: www.wildflowerinn.com. 2059 Darling Hill Rd., Lyndonville. Tel. 802-626-8310. 24 rooms.*

Village Inn of East Burke $$

A good value in the heart of small town Burke, this inn features a fireplaced living room, guest kitchen, great hospitality and humble yet comfortably furnished rooms. Outdoor highlights include a Jacuzzi tub, garden, apiary and brookside picnic area. A former parsonage turned three-bedroom apartment is also on the grounds and makes ideal lodging for large groups. *Info: www.villageinnofeastburke.com. 606 Route 114, East Burke. Tel. 802-626-3161. 6 rooms.*

Juniper's at Wildflower Inn $$-$$$

At one of the area's very best inns, this classy country dining room serves all-natural meats, local beers and vegetarian takes on comfort food in a casual mountain setting. The Kingdom Burger is made from beef raised at Meadow View Farms right down the street. *Info: www.wildflowerinn.com. 3059 Darling Hill Rd., Lyndonville. Tel. 802-626-8310. Breakfast, lunch and dinner Mon.-Sat.*

River Garden Café $$

Tables at this tastefully cozy café overlook the garden, adding ambiance to the River Garden's traditional menu and an excellent wine list featuring 20+ wines by the glass. One of the best little dining experiences in the area, it's most famous for its salad dressings, which are both served and available by the bottle. *Info: 427 Route 114, East Burke. Tel. 802-626-3514. Lunch and dinner Wed.-Sun., brunch Sun. www.rivergardencafe.com.*

Tamarack Grill $$

In the main lodge at the base of the mountain, the Tamarack offers both dining room and pub seating and a menu focused on burgers, grilled meats and hearty fish dinners. It also hosts a live music series and pours a vast selection of local microbrews. *Info: 223 Shelburne Lodge Rd., East Burke. Tel. 802-626-7390. Dinner Tues.-Sun. (Wed.-Sun. in off season), lunch Sat.-Sun. in ski season. www.skiburke.com/tamarackgrill.*

Miss Lyndonville Diner $

The Northeast Kingdom's best breakfast is served out of this old-fashioned diner in Lyndonville. A lengthy menu (with 37 different breakfast choices), hearty portions and low prices keep it popular with locals, so be prepared to wait at peak times. *Info: 686 Broad St., Lyndonville. Tel. 802-626-9890. Breakfast and lunch daily, dinner Wed.-Sun.*

NEWPORT

Cliff Haven Farm B&B $$

Set on 300 acres overlooking Lake Memphremagog, this 19th century farmhouse boasts northernmost Vermont's best combination of value and country character. Carved oak headboards, canopy beds and Vermont Castings fireplaces characterize the down to earth guest rooms, and the surrounding trails, fields and lake views add to the beauty. A full country breakfast is served

SLEEPS & EATS

and features the proprietors' own maple syrup. *Info: www.cliffhavenfarmbedandbreakfast.com. 5463 Lake Rd. Tel. 802-334-2401. 3 rooms.*

East Side Restaurant and Pub $$-$$$

This versatile eatery has a menu nearly as vast as its lakefront views. From salads to prime rib, it satisfies diverse palates, and if you're too full for dessert, its country store will sell you one of its famous pies to go. *Info: 47 Landing St. Tel. 802-334-2340. Breakfast Sat.-Sun., dinner daily. www.eastsiderestaurant.net.*

Lago Trattoria $$

Northernmost Vermont's top Mediterranean option offers outdoor seating in summer and an open kitchen where you can watch chefs execute the wide-ranging Italian menu. House specialties include homemade ravioli and shrimp and clams Amalfi with linguine. *Info: 95 Main St. Tel. 802-334-8222. Dinner daily. www.lagotrattoria.com.*

Newport Natural Foods Café $

The oldest natural foods store in the Northeast Kingdom serves soups, wraps and drinks out of its cozy street side café. It's ideal for a quick warm-up meal, picnic fare or a cup of coffee and a slice of blueberry pie. *Info: 194 Main St. Tel. 802-334-2626. Breakfast, lunch and dinner daily.*

JAY PEAK
Jay Peak Resort $$$

Vermont's northernmost ski resort has a variety of attractive on-mountain lodging options. Right next to the tram and quad, the Hotel Jay is the most convenient and affordable. Condos and townhouse rentals are also available, and most are ski-in, ski-out. Village Condos are the most deluxe option, though all rentals offer modern mountain comforts that are refreshingly free of flash. *Info: www.jaypeakresort.com. 4850 Route 242. Tel. 802-988-2611.*

Phineas Swann B&B $$-$$$

The Jay area's most luxurious B&B is also its most dog-friendly.

A pair of West Highland terriers welcomes you to this plush farmhouse inn, where pets stay free and dog figurines (4,000 in all) are spread  throughout the common areas, which include a dining room, music room and library. Main inn rooms feature flat screens and four-poster beds while the apartment-style River House Suites have private kitchens and Jacuzzi tubs. There is also a pair of luxury suites in the carriage house. Grounds include gardens and a gazebo, and the Trout River borders the property. *Info: www.phineasswann.com. 195 Main St., Montgomery Center. Tel. 802-326-4306. 7 rooms.*

Rendezvous B&B $-$$
Set on 11 acres 18 miles from Jay Peak in Lowell, this 19th century white farmhouse exudes warmth from the woodburning stove in the parlor to the homemade afghans in the bedrooms. Antique oak furniture, copious bookshelves, a full breakfast and mountain views add further comfort. *Info: www.rendezvousbandb.net. 2507 Route 100, Lowell. Tel. 802-744-2085. 3 rooms.*

Woodshed Lodge $-$$
This hilltop inn 10 minutes from Jay provides basic rooms with country décor and shared or private bath. Breakfast and dinner are both served in the dining room and offer flavor, value and camaraderie. Dietary requests are happily satisfied. *Info: www.woodshedlodge.com. Woodshed Rd. off Route 242. Tel. 800-495-4445. 7 rooms.*

North Troy Inn $
Just a mile from the Canadian border and 10 miles from Jay, this 1880s Victorian home offers classic farmhouse accommodations at budget rates. Rooms are simply furnished yet welcoming, and a full organic breakfast is provided. *Info: www.northtroyinn.com. 35 Route 243, N. Troy. Tel. 802-988-2527. 5 rooms.*

SLEEPS & EATS

Valhalla Restaurant and Pub at the Inglenook Lodge $$-$$$
The best of the area's limited restaurant options, the Inglenook's dining room is reminiscent of a European ski lodge, both in terms of décor and the German-American hybrid menu that changes nightly. *Info: 3866 Route 242. Tel. 802-988-2880. Breakfast and dinner daily. www.inglenookvermont.com.*

The Belfry $-$$
This cozy pub occupies a renovated former school house building south of Jay in Montgomery Center. It's popular with locals and tourists alike for its blackboard specials, seafood dishes and a lively bar scene. *Info: Route 242, Montgomery. Tel. 802-326-4400. Dinner daily.*

BEST SHOPPING

St. Johnsbury
St. Johnsbury is the Kingdom's commercial hub and is pretty much the only town where you can spend much more than an hour or two shopping. Its stores, including **Kingdom Outdoors** and the **Northeast Kingdom Artisans Guild and Gallery**, are clustered along **Railroad Street**.

Elsewhere in the Kingdom
Newport, to the Kingdom's far north, is the only other major town in the area. Its small consumer district starts (and ends) with Main Street.

The Kingdom's lack of commercial centers doesn't mean a lack of interesting shopping,

though. Country stores, farm stands and local crafters can be found along obscure country roads and in the Kingdom's smallest towns. To cite just a few, the **Castle Shoppe** antiquery in Irasburg is a one-of-a-kind vintage outlet; the **Galaxy bookshop** (*7 Mill St.*) in Hardwick is one of the state's great little booksellers; and **Willey's** in Greensboro (*7 Breezy Ave.*) and **Bailey's and Burke** in East Burke (*466 Route Rt. 114*) are two of the state's best country stores. The most popular shop in all the Kingdom may be the **Cabot Cheese Cooperative factory store**

SHOPPING

in Cabot Village (*2878 Main St., Tel. 800-837-4261*), long a favorite stop for its dairy products and Vermont spe-

cialty food items. For more information on shopping, visit *www.nekchamber.org.*

VERMONT CORN MAZE

Corn mazes – or trails lined with 10-foot tall walls of corn – are a unique farm attraction that appear throughout the state. Open August to October, the **Vermont Corn Maze** in Danville (*1404 Wheelock Rd., Tel. 802-748-1399*) is among the best. Its seven-acre maze has two miles of trails, takes at least an hour to traverse and can be visited by daylight or starlight. **Info**: *www.vermontcornmaze.com.*

BEST NIGHTLIFE & ENTERTAINMENT

In many cases, the Kingdom's best restaurants double as evening hangouts. **Elements Food and Spirit** in St. Johnsbury (*98 Mill St, Tel. 802-748-8400*) and **Claire's** in Hardwick (*41 S. Main St., Tel. 802-472-7053*) both have handsome bar areas with the same appeal as their progressive cuisine. The Kingdom's best brewpub is in Lyndonville, where the **Trout River Brewing Company** on Route 5 (*Tel. 802-626-9396*) serves sourdough pizzas and its line of craft beers on weekends.

Neither Burke nor Jay have après-ski scenes to rival the resorts to the south. Nevertheless, there are low-key spots to unwind post-slopes,

from Jay's **Lodge Pub n' Grill** to the **Tamarack Grill** at Burke. Both offer regular live music, casual bar fare and collegial atmosphere.

Performing arts venues in the Kingdom are few, but those that exist make an impression. **Bread and Puppet Theater's summer pageants** in Glover (*753 Heights Rd., Tel. 802-525-3031*) are performance-art extravaganzas not to be missed (*see sidebar on next page*). The **Haskell Opera House** near the Canadian border in Derby Line (*93 Caswell Ave., Tel. 802-873-3022*) is a small gem that presents both music and theater productions. On a

NIGHTLIFE & ENTERTAINMENT

NIGHTLIFE & ENTERTAINMENT

smaller scale, the **Catamount Arts Center** (*115 Eastern Ave., Tel. 802-748-2600*) in St. Johnsbury hosts a popular film series and jazz concerts on weekends.

BREAD & PUPPET THEATER

Known for its left-wing politics and extraordinarily large-scale paper mache puppets, the **Bread and Puppet Theater** has been presenting its idiosyncratically brilliant pageants in the Vermont hills since the 1970s. Blending storytelling with music, puppetry and themes of equality and peace, its summertime performances are mandatory viewing, as is the ramshackle hay barn turned puppet museum, with its panoply of faces peering out from the rafters. *Info: 753 Heights Rd., Glover. Open daily 10 am-5 pm May-Oct., performances July-Aug. Admission free. Tel. 802-525-1271. www.breadandpuppet.org.*

BEST SPORTS & RECREATION

The Kingdom's range of outdoor recreation is unmatched anywhere in the region. With hundreds of lakes, mountains and miles of forested terrain, the only limits on sporting endeavors here are stamina and imagination.

In the southern part of the Kingdom, the **Groton State Forest's** 25,000 acres encompass numerous state parks, from secluded **Kettle Pond State Park** (*Tel. 802-426-3042*) to **Stillwater State Park** on Lake Groton (*Tel. 802-584-3822*). **Ricker Pond State Park** (*Tel. 802-584-3821*) has excellent camping facilities, and the Wells River trail in **New Discovery State Park** (*Tel. 802-426-3042*) offers some of the forest's best hiking, biking and horseback riding. Eighty more miles of trails await hikers and skiers at the **Craftsbury Outdoor Center** (*535 Lost Nation Rd., Tel. 802-586-7767*). It's also a top destination for sculling.

The state's largest recreational trail network – with some of the best mountain biking terrain anywhere in the world – is **Kingdom Trails** in Burke (*www.kingdomtrails.org*). Hiking and snowshoeing are also popular pursuits; pick up a trail guide or arrange a tour at **East Burke Sports** (*439 Route 114, Tel. 802-626-3215*) before heading out. You can also buy a mandatory trail access pass here or at the welcome center located behind the **Bailey's and Burke General Store** (*466 Route 114*).

Not far from Burke, the **Lake Willoughby area** is another versatile recreational paradise, with great public beaches, hiking and climbing in a dramatic, fjord-like setting. Three hours top to bottom, the **Pisgah Trail** (trailhead a half-mile south of the lake) is the most steeply revelatory trek here, though the moderate **Herbert Hawkes Trail** on **Mt. Hor** makes a spectacular ascent above Willoughby too. Countless other gorgeous lakes dot the area too. **Seymour Lake** outside Morgan; **Island Pond** in Brighton; **Caspian Lake** near Greensboro; and **Lake Memphremagog** in Newport are just a few of the Lake Region's best spots for kayaking, swimming, boating and fishing.

If you're looking for something even more adventurous, tour operators offer all sorts of novel outdoor experiences. You can rock climb or ice climb in the Lake Willoughby area with **Vermont Adventure Tours** (*Tel. 802-773-3343*). They also lead hiking, fly fishing and paddling expeditions. **Hardscrabble Mountain Tours** (*Tel. 802-626-9895*) offers sled dog runs and guided snowshoe hikes around Caledonia County. Even farms in the region have recreational potential. **Perry Farm** in Brownington (*509 Dutton Brook Ln., Tel. 802-754-2396*) is one of many offering horseback rides and sleigh rides, and a third-generation dairy farm in Danville (*1404 Wheelock Rd.,*

Tel. 802-748-1399) attracts visitors with its startlingly unique seven-acre Vermont Corn Maze.

The nightlife may not be wild at the Kingdom's ski resorts, but the terrain sure is. **Burke Mountain** (*off Route 114, www.skiburke.com*) has a 2,000-foot vertical drop, 45 trails, four terrain parks and a top Nordic center that are popular with locals and visitors alike. To the far north, **Jay Peak** (*off Route 242, www.jaypeakresort.com*) gets more snow than any other New England ski area. Advanced glades like Valhalla and Beaver Pond entice expert skiers, though skate-ski and snowshoeing trails and affordable instruction lure skiers of all stripes.

When all that snow melts, you can also hike the Long Trail up Jay Peak or play a round of golf at the region's newest championship golf course. You can also hit the links throughout the Kingdom, from the **St. Johnsbury Country Club** (*off Route 5, Tel. 802-748-9894*) to the Caspian Lake-overlooking **Mountain View** course in Greensboro (*112 Country Club Rd., Tel. 802-533-7477*).

10. PRACTICAL MATTERS

GETTING TO VERMONT

Flying to Vermont

Most flights in and out of Vermont go through **Burlington International Airport**. The state's only major airport is serviced by seven major airlines: Air Tran, Continental, Delta, JetBlue, Northwest, USAir and United. Relatively small and streamlined, Burlington International is a great little airport, welcoming as much for its recent $15 million makeover as for the information kiosk that's staffed daily from 9 am to midnight. Rental car, taxi and local bus service can all be accessed from the airport terminal. *Info: Tel. 802-863-1889, www.burlingtonintlairport.com.*

Rutland–Southern Vermont Regional Airport is the state's other accessible air destination. Cape Air flies to Rutland daily from Boston's Logan Airport, and the quick one-hour flight is worth exploring if you're traveling to the central part of the state.

Depending on where you're traveling from, flying directly to Vermont may be expensive or time-consuming. Other nearby options include Manchester, NH (2 hours from eastern Vermont and serviced by Southwest Airlines); Boston, MA (2 1/2 hours from eastern Vermont); Montréal, QC (75 minutes from the Vermont border and 2 hours from Burlington); Albany, NY (45 minutes from southwestern Vermont); and Hartford, CT (1 1/2 hours from southeastern Vermont).

By Car

A car is by far the best way to get around Vermont once you're there, so if you're traveling from anywhere nearby, you may as well bring your own. Drivers will find **tourist information/welcome centers** at many entry points, including White River Junction, Guilford (outside Brattleboro) and along the Canadian border.

If you're driving into Vermont from Canada, you will have to pass through customs. For information on that process see the Passports & Visas section later in this chapter.

If you're on a tight schedule or plan to cross the border during a

particularly busy travel time, you can get information on the wait times at various border crossings at the following web sites:
* apps.cbp.gov/bwt (US)
* www.cbsa-asfc.gc.ca/general/ times/menu-f.html (CA).

By Train
AMTRAK's Vermonter runs from Washington, D.C. to St. Albans in northwest Vermont. Start to finish it's a 13 3/4 hour journey, but you don't necessarily have to ride it all the way. The Vermonter passes through Philadelphia, New York, Hartford and many other northeast towns en route, and it also makes nine stops in Vermont on its way upstate.

Another AMTRAK train, the **Ethan Allen Express**, provides daily service between New York City and Rutland. The 5 1/2 trip leads through the Hudson Valley, Albany and Saratoga, and Fair Haven and Rutland are its lone stops in Vermont.

Info: Tel. 800-872-7245, www.amtrak.com.

By Bus
Greyhound provides bus service linking Vermont with major East Coast cities such as New York, Boston and Montréal. Regional service is also provided from other points in New England. *Info: Tel. 800-231-2222, www.greyhound.com.*

Traveling by bus from Canada, be advised that you will have to pass through Customs – occasionally a lengthy process at peak times or when the bus is full.

By Boat
Ferry service across Lake Champlain links eastern New York State with Vermont and provides wonderful views of the lake, the Adirondacks and the Green Mountains in the process.

Lake Champlain Ferries travels from Port Kent, NY to King Street Dock in Burlington from late May through mid-October. The one-hour trip costs $17.50 one way, $32.75 round trip for cars and $4.95 one way, $9.30 round trip for pedestrians. Credits cards are accepted.

Lake Champlain Ferries also provides year-round service between Plattsburgh, NY and Grand Isle, VT (12 minutes) and between Essex, NY and Charlotte, VT (20 minutes). Fares are cash only and cost $9.50 one way, $18 round trip for cars and $3.75 one way, $6.25 round trip for pedestrians. *Info: Tel. 802-864-9804, www.ferries.com.*

The **Fort Ticonderoga Ferry** also connects New York with Vermont via Larabees Point and Shoreham. The seven minute crossings cost $8 one way, $14 round trip for cars, $1 each way for pedestrians. The ferry makes three trips per hour and runs from mid-May through mid-October. *Info: Tel. 802-897-7999, www.middlebury.org/tiferry.*

GETTING AROUND VERMONT
By Car
Driving is by far the most efficient way to travel around Vermont. Two major interstates and an easily navigable network of state highways thoroughly connect all corners of the state, and scenic backroad driving is one of the chief thrills of traveling through it.

Speed limits rise to 65 mph on Vermont interstates but go down significantly on back roads. They can change frequently as you go in and out of towns, so stay alert. Gas stations can also be few and far between when traveling off main roads. Never let your tank get too low, particularly when driving through the more remote reaches of the Northeast Kingdom. Just because a town is on the map doesn't mean it has a gas station. Also exercise caution when driving in inclement weather. For up to date information on driving conditions call 511 or visit 511.vermont.gov.

If you plan to rent a car upon arrival, you'll need a valid driver's license with photo ID and a major credit card. Most companies impose an age minimum of 25 years, with some permitting drivers ages 21-25 with an extra charge. Always book in advance.

If you're planning to rent a car upon arrival, the following rental car companies **operate out of Burlington International Airport**:
• Alamo: *Tel. 800-327-9633*
• Avis: *Tel. 800-331-1212*
• Budget: *Tel. 800-527-0700*
• Enterprise: *Tel. 800-325-8007*
• Hertz: *Tel. 800-654-3131*
• National: *Tel. 800-227-7368*

By Train
AMTRAK's Vermonter train follows the state's eastern border from Brattleboro up to White River Junction, stopping in Bellows Falls, Claremont and Windsor before turning northwest and stopping in Randolph, Montpelier-Barre, Waterbury-Stowe and Burlington on its way to St. Albans. En route, you can take advantage of the unique **Trails & Rails program**, an educational partnership between

Amtrak and the National Park Service that fosters appreciation of the area's natural and cultural heritage. *Info: Tel. 800-872-7245, www.nps.gov/trails&rails.*

AMTRAK's other Vermont train, the **Ethan Allen Express**, stops in Rutland, and a trio of tourist trains traverses the state during summer and fall. More scenic novelty than serious transportation option, the **Green Mountain Railroad** offers three vintage routes: the Green Mountain Flyer between Bellows Falls and Chester; the White River Flyer between White River Junction, Thetford and Montshire; and the Champlain Valley Flyer between Burlington and Charlotte. *Info: Tel. 802-463-3069, www.rails-vt.com.*

By Bus

Greyhound maintains stations in Bellows Falls, Brattleboro, Burlington, Montpelier and White River Junction. Some towns and resorts also offer local or shuttle bus service between major attractions and destinations. *Info: Tel. 800-231-2222, www.greyhound.com.*

BUSINESS HOURS

Though 9 to 5 is status quo for shops and banks, many Vermont businesses observe seasonal hours. This often involves

THE LONG TRAIL

Vermont's famed **Long Trail** has 440 miles of trails and follows the ridge of the Green Mountains through the entire state, from Massachusetts to Canada. Half the trail runs through the **Green Mountain National Forest**, and its entire length is maintained by the **Green Mountain Club** (GMC), which built the trail – the oldest long distance trail in the country – between 1910 and 1930. Amateur and expert hikers enjoy its varied terrain (woods, mountains, ponds), and shelters every five to seven miles provide respite. *Info: www.greenmountainclub.org.*

extended hours in summer and fall and abbreviated ones the rest of the year. Many businesses are open on a limited basis in winter and some – including some museums and tourist attractions – close altogether. It's always best to call ahead, especially if you're traveling off season.

CLIMATE & WEATHER

Vermont enjoys all four seasons – six seasons, in fact, if you include "mud season" in early spring and "stick season" in late fall. The former follows the spring thaw and is the bane of dirt roads everywhere while anyone who's gone leaf peeping a little too late in the season knows all about the latter.

For a state with a brr-inducing reputation, Vermont's climate is pleasingly diverse. Spring is crisp; summer is pleasantly balmy; autumn means leaves; and winter is sublimely snowy – all just as they should be. If you've come for the snow, it generally begins falling in late November and continues through March. **December, January and February routinely get more than 20 inches of snow** in all but the southernmost parts of the state. The far north gets particularly frigid in winter – often 10 degrees or more colder than the south. Check a site like *weather.com* before you leave home.

DRINKING & SMOKING

As in the rest of the country, the legal drinking age in Vermont is 21. Be prepared to show picture ID. By law smoking is prohibited in all restaurants and bars, with the exception of those with outdoor seating.

MAPLE SYRUP & SUGARING

Vermont produces more than **400,000 gallons of maple syrup annually** – more than one-third of American production. Prime maple season runs from February to April, depending on the region. **Sugarhouses** can be visited throughout the state, and the **Vermont Maple Foundation's** Web site, *www.vtmaple.org*, includes a comprehensive list broken down by county.

You might think grades of syrup have to do with quality, but distinctions such as Fancy and Grade A dark are really just a matter of taste. Fancy grade syrup is lighter and subtler while darker grades have a stronger flavor and are best for baking. Grade B syrups are darker than Grade A.

EMERGENCIES & SAFETY

Coordinated emergency services throughout Vermont can be reached by dialing 911. **Vermont Emergency Management** also maintains a toll-free hotline for developing emergencies. *Info: Tel. 800-347-0488.*

There are few vacation destinations in the United States that are as safe as Vermont. Violent crime is rare, and if someone suddenly comes up behind you, it's much more likely that they need directions than that they're after your wallet. Even so, the usual safety measures still apply. Be aware of your surroundings. Use caution late at night. Keep money hidden. Never leave possessions exposed in your car. Store valuables in your hotel safe, and always keep doors locked and bolted when in your room.

FESTIVALS, HOLIDAYS & CONVENTIONS

Should your visit coincide with the holidays or a major festival, plan on making reservations earlier than you otherwise would.

Following is a brief list of some of Vermont's most popular seasonal attractions.

January: Vermont Farm Show (Barre)

February: Winter carnivals (Brattleboro, Burlington, Middlebury)

March: Green Mountain Film Festival (Montpelier); Vermont Flower Show (Burlington)

April: Vermont Maple Festival (St. Albans)

May: Vermont Chocolate Show (Essex)

June: Discover Jazzfest (Burlington); Chew-Chew Food and Music Festival (Burlington); Vermont Dairy Festival (Enosburg Falls); Strolling of the Heifers (Brattleboro); Killington Music Festival

July: Vermont Brewers' Festival (Burlington); Champlain Shakespeare Festival (Burlington); Vermont Mozart Festival (Burlington); Marlboro Music Festival (July/August); Killington Wine Festival

August: Champlain Valley Folk Festival (Ferrisburgh); Festival of Fools (Burlington); Champlain Valley Fair (Essex); Deerfield Valley Blueberry Festival (Wilmington)

September: Vermont State Fair (Rutland); Vermont Life Wine and Harvest Festival (Wilmington); Plymouth Cheese and Harvest Festival; Tunbridge World's Fair

October: Applefest (South Hero); Dummerston Apple Pie Festival; Festival 05301 (Brattleboro); Newfane

Heritage Festival; Stowe Foliage Arts & Crafts Festival
November: Festival of Vermont Crafters (Barre); Festival of Sweets (Burlington)
December: First Night (Burlington)

INTERNET ACCESS

Most resorts and many hotels and inns offer in-room Internet access, whether Wi-Fi or Ethernet; some charge for the privilege. Local coffeeshops and libraries often offer free Internet access, and copy shops in major towns also offer computers and Internet access for a nominal sum.

LANGUAGE

English is spoken in Vermont, though in the far north you may hear French spoken along the border with Québec.

MONEY, BANKING & TAXES

ATMs are easy to find in cities and larger towns and are increasingly prevalent at small town general stores and filling stations. They remain the best way to access cash. Even with bank surcharges, they preclude the need to carry large amounts of cash while offering international travelers the best exchange rates. Exchanging foreign currency at the airport and major hotels is possible but generally results in unfavorable

SKI SEASON

Vermont's ski season can start as soon as the beginning of November, although **Thanksgiving weekend** is the average opening date for the majority of resorts. Most close for the season sometime in April, though northern mountains such as Jay often remain open later.

You can call or visit most ski areas' Web sites for updates on mountain conditions. Try *www.skivermont.com* for a complete list of alpine and cross-country conditions, including recent snowfall stats and the number of lifts and trails in operation.

rates. Credit cards are widely accepted and should be used for major purchases. In smaller towns many establishments only accept cash, so be sure to have some in your wallet before heading off the beaten path. Traveler's checks are also widely accepted, though you may be asked to provide identification first.

Vermont sales tax is six percent. Some towns such as Killington have a local 1 percent option tax. There is also a **nine percent state tax on meals and lodging.**

PASSPORTS & VISAS

If you're driving into Vermont from Canada, you will pass through Customs. All travelers entering the United States must show proof of citizenship such as a birth certificate or passport **and** a photo ID. A driver's license is no longer sufficient identification by itself.

If visiting from abroad, you will need a passport and, in many cases, a visa to enter the United States. For detailed information, contact the American embassy in your own country or your own immigration authorities. United States Customs also imposes limits on what you can carry with you in and out of the country. When in doubt, contact the U.S. Customs Service. *Info:Tel.* 877-227-5511, *www.cbp.gov.*

POSTAL SERVICES

Post offices can be found in major towns as well as in many smaller ones. Most operate between 8am and 5pm Monday through Friday, with some variation. Most have Saturday morning hours as well. Many post offices in small towns close for an hour around midday. You can purchase stamps at any post office as well as at hotels and drug stores.

SENIOR CITIZENS

Many places offer senior citizen discounts. Some hotels offer special packages for seniors, and many ski resorts, including Killington, Jay and Mad River Glen, offer discounted passes. Smugglers' Notch even lets visitors 70 and older ski for free.

TELEPHONES

All of Vermont is within the **802 area code.** To make a local call, dial the area code and then the number. To make an international call, dial 011 plus the area code and number. Dial 411 for information. Though cell phones are making them harder to find, pay phones can still be accessed in most towns. Be careful when making calls from your hotel room. Many have exorbitant rates, so check printed in-room information or dial the front desk to ask first.

TIME

Vermont is in the Eastern Time Zone and observes Daylight Savings Time.

TIPPING

A tip of 20% is now customary in restaurants, with 15% now on the low end. If your party is a large one, some restaurants will automatically add the tip to your bill, so check before you pay. At bars, $1 per drink or $2 per round is a good rule of thumb. A couple of dollars suffices for taxi drivers, with 15-20% for longer rides. Tip doormen and bell staff at hotels, from $1 for minor assistance to a few dollars for bag service. Valet parking attendants also get a dollar or two.

TOURIST INFORMATION

The State of Vermont maintains a comprehensive web Site – www.vermontvacation.com – with lots of information on services, transportation and things to do. It's helpful both before and during your trip.

Other helpful online sources:
• www.vermont.gov
• www.vtchamber.com
• www.skivermont.com
• www.vtstateparks.com
• www.historicvermont.org

Staffed by friendly Vermonters, there are **seven welcome centers** at various state entry points as well as 13 information centers strategically placed in towns and along major thoroughfares. Vermont's information centers assist an estimated 11,000 people each day. Some towns offer their own visitor information services as well.

WATER

Water from Vermont springs is marketed nationwide as some of the purest and best tasting in the land. You may find water straight from the tap here preferable to the filtered water you drink at home. Bottled water is also widely available throughout Vermont. Whatever your water source, drink lots of it when out and about. Never drink directly from mountain streams.

INDEX

TravelNotes

Things Change!

Phone numbers, prices, addresses, quality of service – all change. If you come across any new information, let us know. No item is too small! Contact us at :

jopenroad@aol.com
or
www.openroadguides.com

PHOTO CREDITS

Front cover image©Ken Traub. Pages 1-3©Jeff Newcomer/ PatridgeBrookReflections.com

The following images are from flickr.com: pp. 5, 113, 114, 131: cogdogblog; pp. 8, 12: allyrose18; pp. 9, 18, 34: PhillipC; p. 11: Chrissy Olson; p. 14: Kingfox; p. 17: Ken30684; p. 24: Joe Shlabotnik; p. 25: cwbuecheler; p. 26: jsmuns; p. 27: pincusvt; p. 28 right: Imaji; p. 28 left: lowjumpingfrog; p. 44:@dens; pp. 45, 76, 224: dvs; p. 46: sskennel; p. 47: Paraflyer; p. 50: WalkingGeek; pp. 51, 188: Tony the Misfit; p. 55: EandJsFilmCrew; p. 77: j_piepkorn65; p. 78: dicktay2000; p.80: Robert W. Leslie; pp.81, 83: SnapsterMax; p. 82: Bob Simari; pp. 84, 91, 103, 179: Iceburns; pp. 85, 137, 229: NearDC (Chad Connell); p. 86: Seamus Murray; p. 89: Stefan Mendelsohn (Germany); p. 104: Derek Purdy; p. 107: LDHNY; pp. 117, 119, 136: dvs; p. 120: Redacted; p. 144: eralon; p. 145: VickieVictoria; pp. 149, 192: reed_flickr; p. 170: snappybex; p. 177: sleepyneko; p. 186: bobw235; p. 189: Savannah Grandfather; p. 190: atalou; p. 197: redjar; p. 200: bcpnyc; p. 202: moneydick; p. 227: phoosh.

The following photos are from wikimedia commons: p. 52: Skkezix1000; p. 54: Rolf Muller; p. 140: Jared C. Benedict; p. 152: Dudesleeper; p. 193: Jessamyn West; p. 196: Nat Tripp; p. 218: Walter Wantman;

The following photos are from Brian Potter: pp. 10, 19, 20, 43, 72, 115, 146, 159, 160, 162, 167, 183, 225.

The following photos are from Killington Resort: back cover and pp 108, 120, 134. *The following photos are from The Equinox Hotel:* p 57, 64. *The following photo is from Tom O'Donnell:* pp. 59, 90. *The following photo is from PowderPassport.com:* p. 110. *The following photo is from sugarbush.com:* p. 133. *The following photo is from stowe.com:* p. 150. *The following photos are from Smuggler's Notch:* pp. 164, 166. *The following photos are from Jim Thompson, Vermont Lenses:* pp. 199, 220. *The following photo is from jaypeakresort.com:* p. 205.

Note: the use of these photos does not represent an endorsement of this book or any services listed within by any of the photographers listed above.

Open Road Publishing

Open Road's *Best Of* guides match the time you *really* have for your vacation with the right amount of information you need for your perfect trip! No fluff, just the best things to do and see, the best places to stay and eat. Includes one-day, weekend, one-week and two-week trip ideas. Now what could be more perfect than that?

Best Of Guides

Open Road's Best of Vermont, $14.95
Open Road's Best of Arizona, $14.95
Open Road's Best of The Florida Keys, $14.95
Open Road's Best of Las Vegas, $14.95
Open Road's Best of New York City, $14.95
Open Road's Best of Southern California, $14.95
Open Road's Best of Northern California, $14.95
Open Road's Best of the Bahamas, $14.95
Open Road's Best of Bermuda, $14.95
Open Road's Best of Belize, $14.95
Open Road's Best of Costa Rica, $14.95
Open Road's Best of Honduras, $14.95

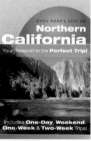

Open Road's Best of Panama, $14.95
Open Road's Best of Guatemala, $14.95
Open Road's Best of Ireland, $14.95
Open Road's Best of Italy, $16.95
Open Road's Best of Paris, $12.95
Open Road's Best of Provence &
    The French Riviera, $14.95
Open Road's Best of Spain, $14.95

Family Travel Guides

Open Road's Italy with Kids, $16.95
Open Road's Paris with Kids, $16.95
Open Road's Caribbean with Kids, $14.95
Open Road's London with Kids, $14.95
Open Road's New York City with Kids, $14.95
Open Road's Best National Parks With Kids, $14.95
Open Road's Washington, DC with Kids, $14.95
Open Road's Hawaii with Kids, $14.95

Order now at **www.openroadguides.com**